Just a Kid from Swampoodle to Vietnam

Edmond J. Cubbage

A Collection of Short Stories of Soldiers and Events about My Time in the Service and the Year Serving My Country in Vietnam, 1965-67.

Copyright © 2020 Edmond and Elaine Cubbage.

All rights reserved. This book or any portion thereof may not be reproduced or used in any manner whatsoever without the express written permission of the publisher except for the use of brief quotations in a book review.

Printed by Edmond and Elaine Cubbage, in the United States of America.

First printing, 2020.

Copyright © 2020 Edmond and Elaine Cubbage. All rights reserved. No part of this publication may be reproduced, distributed, or transmitted in any form or by any means, including photocopying, recording, or other electronic or mechanical methods, without the prior written permission of the publisher, except in the case of brief quotations embodied in critical reviews and certain other noncommercial uses permitted by copyright law. For permission requests, write to the publisher, addressed "Attention: Permissions Coordinator," at the address below.

ISBN: 979-8-64969473-5 (Paperback)

Front cover by Elaine Cubbage.

Book design by Elaine Cubbage.

Dedication

To all my friends who died in Vietnam.
Freedom is not free; our freedom was paid for
by my friends who made the ultimate sacrifice.

Table of Contents

"Do I remember basic training?" and here it goes:..........1

Boot Camp, Fort Jackson, South Carolina, August 1, 1965 2

The Army Tears You Down, Then Builds You Back Up! 3

Meals 4

You Are a Proud Soldier...5

Advance Infantry Training, Fort Gordon, Georgia 7

Buffing the Floor...9

Airborne Training, Fort Benning, Georgia, December, 1965 12

Back to Fort Benning, GA., Airborne Training 16

My Going Away Party 20

Friends as Close as Brothers 21

Woodhouse and I, in AIT and Airborne Training..........22

Woodhouse and I, in Vietnam 23

Bell's Ominous Premonition, February, 1966 25

Hawaii, February 21, 1966	26
This was the beginning of a bad year…	28
Camp Alpha, Vietnam, February 22, 1966	28
Phuoc Vinh, Vietnam, February 26, 1966	30
Guys We Met in Our Tent	31
Building Bunkers	32
Swimming	33
Operation Junction City	35
Operation Birmingham	36
Shit Houses	39
The EM Club	41
Another Operation	43
Pfc Richard Recupero	43
Stand on Your Toes, LBJ	46
Beer	47
A Thief in the Night	48
Lou Rivera, a Good Friend	50
The Body Count	52

On Patrol in the Jungles 53

Point Man 54

Beer Cans, Flip Flops and Cool Aid 56

On Patrol 57

Sergeant Lewis Jackson 59

MPs and an Article 15 61

Leg Cramps 66

Battle of Minh Thanh Road, July 9, 1966 67

The Wire 71

Highway 13, Thunder Road, Ambush Alley 73

Medic Vernie Williams 74

"Conversion.... From Combat Medic to Combat Infantryman" 75

The Mamasan 81

I Had a Good Dog 82

Johnny Moore, My Native American Friend 86

The Weather, Red Ants, and Wait-A-Minute Bushes 89

Low-Grade Gunpowder 92

.50 Caliber Machine Gun 92

I Met Friends from Swampoodle in Vietnam 94

Sgt. Tahike, Sgt. Jackson, Sgt. DeJean, Sgt. Rivera.....100

TK Stone 100

The Battle of Bong Trang, August 25, 1966 104

The Longest Day of My Life 104

"The Battle of Bong Trang" in My Friend's Own Words
....113

Chuck Mundahl, August 25, 1966 113

Worthless Fat Sergeant..120

A Visit from My Friend, "The Fogue Guy" 122

I Visit my Friend, "The Fogue Guy" in Bien Hoa 126

The Tunnel 128

"We Are in a Hostile Area" 130

The Big Dust Off..132

No Bob Hope Show, December, 1966..........................134

The German Shepherd 136

I'm Short 138

Time to Go Home...141

No Welcome Home Parade for Our Vietnam War
Veterans 143

Freedom Is Not Free 143

Thank You for Your Service 145

Getting Closer to Home 150

Finally, Home Sweet Home 151

Horn and Hardart..152

Freedom is not free; our freedom was paid for by my
friends. 157

Effects of the Vietnam War on Joseph M. Egan 157

Hall of Honor...161

Image Citations 163

Collection of Short Stories of Soldiers and Events about

My Time in the Service & the Year Serving My Country in Vietnam.

Just Another Kid from Swampoodle to Vietnam

This book was started by my wife, Elaine, asking me,

"Do I remember basic training?" and here it goes:

As I got on the bus at 401 North Broad Street, Philadelphia, PA. I was with Frank Gallagher, and Billy Trampe, who were also from Swampoodle.

We got on the train at 30th Street and we went to Washington DC. We had a three-hour delay. So, we went out to a bar. We were allowed to drink alcohol at 18 years old in Washington DC. We partied for three hours, then got back on the train and went to Fort Jackson, South Carolina. Frank Gallagher went to the 4th Infantry and he made it back home and is now living in North Wildwood.

Boot Camp, Fort Jackson, South Carolina, August 1, 1965

The sergeants were outside waiting for us. As soon as we pulled up the sergeants began yelling, "Get off the bus now, get off the bus now. The last one off the bus is going to give me some pushups." Billy Trampe started laughing and said, "Oh shit, they are starting already." We sort of knew they were going to start giving us a hard time. Everyone hustled off the bus. They said, "We are going to be your mothers now. You never listened to your mother, but you are going to listen to us. We will tell you when to eat, when to sleep, when to walk and when to run. We are going to watch you like your mothers never watched you before. You are in the military now." They got us into formation and they marched us up to the supply room. They gave us our boots and our fatigues. We yelled out what size we were, and they threw them over to us. We exchanged them the next day if they did not fit. They also gave us a crew cut, goodbye beautiful auburn hair. The next day the sergeants came in around 5:30 am, banging on the beds with a stick and the lid of a trash can. "Alright we are going for a run. Get your ass out of the bunk." It was dark outside and when we got back, it was light out. We started, PT (physical training) for one or two hours. We did hundreds of jumping jacks, push-ups, running in place, sit ups, etc. Then, we went to breakfast. You had to know your serial number, US 52631989. If you didn't know it or if you hesitated, they made you go to the back of the line. There were at least two hundred guys in line, you went behind all of them.

The Army Tears You Down, Then Builds You Back Up!

The sergeant came into our room the next morning yelling, "You are a lazy piece of shit, get out of bed. We are going to do PT." One guy laughed and the sergeant ran over to him and screamed in his face, "You worthless piece of shit, what are you laughing at? I want you to go outside and stick your head out and yell to the world that you are a f... idiot, and you don't know what you are doing." He went outside and yelled, "I am a f... idiot, and I don't know what I am doing." He came back in and the sergeant said, "Don't you feel good, you told the world that you are a f... idiot, and you don't know what you are doing. Don't you feel good now, boy?"

The sergeant saw another guy laughing and he ran over and screamed at him, "Go outside and tell the world you are a bigger idiot because you just got your sergeant mad at you, and now you are going to get everyone in your platoon mad at you too. The only thing that is going to make me happy is… running." The soldier went outside and yelled exactly what the sergeant said. When he came back in, the sergeant said, "You have five minutes to get outside." So, we scrambled to get our fatigues and boots on. We didn't want to be the last one outside, because the last one out had to do pushups.

Meals

You go to breakfast after PT. You get in line and take a tray. The servers gave you bacon, eggs, sausage, chipped beef, grits, oatmeal, milk, coffee, and orange juice. It was a better breakfast than I ever had at home. This was the first time I ever ate chipped beef for breakfast, I always thought it was for dinner.

The sergeants would come in while you were eating and start yelling at people. If you looked up, they would run over, grab your tray, and tell you to get out. That happened to me once, I looked up and they ran over and grabbed my dinner tray, and yelled "Outside, if you have time enough to look around then you are not hungry, get out of here, now!" I waited outside until they came out. Sometimes they would yell, "Seconds!" and you would run back inside and eat.

You Are a Proud Soldier

The sergeants tear you down by saying, "You are dirt, you are slime, you are the worst thing that crawls on this earth." Then by the end of eight weeks of training, they build you back up and you become a proud soldier. You have a graduation parade and you wear your dress uniform. You are physically and mentally stronger. You are no longer slime; you are a **SOLDIER.** You are proud of the soldier you have become.

Some of the things you have to do to graduate are: you have to shimmy across a rope over a stream. Sergeants were there to throw a rope to you, if you didn't know how to swim. You stayed wet all day, if you fell in.

At night you had to "escape an invasion." They taught you how to read a map, in order to get from one place to the next. Other soldiers would try to catch you. They would intimidate you, beat you with belts, and throw water on you, just like the enemy would do. The training was rugged. They taught you how to fight and how to survive in the woods. They would teach you which plants and bugs you can eat, and which ones to stay away from, how to kill animals, and how to survive in the wilderness. They were experiences that you didn't know anything about, especially if you were from the big city.

August, 1965, President Johnson doubled the draft and we were the first doubled class that graduated with 500 soldiers. They didn't have room for us. We had to set up our own tent, that was as big as a house. We wore fatigues for training and dress uniform when we went home.

When you serve in the military, you are taught discipline. We did what was asked of us, and we looked after those that we served with. After we graduated from Basic Training, we became a **Proud SOLDIER!**

Advance Infantry Training
Fort Gordon, Georgia, October, 1965

I left Boot Camp in Fort Jackson, South Carolina to go to **AIT, Advance Infantry Training** in Fort Gordon, Georgia.

They train you with rifles: M14, M16, AR15, 45, M60 machine gun, and different types of mortars. You learn how to take them apart, put them back together again, and how to keep them clean. If you run out of cleaning stuff you would use your toothbrush or your underwear to clean them. The sergeants would say, "You can do without your teeth because you can chop your food up and drink from a straw, even soup if it is necessary, but you can't do without your weapon. Your life depends on your weapon. You don't need a tooth brush but you do need your weapon.

When you are in formation the sergeant would say, "When you go into combat, look to the right of you, look to the left of you, one of you or both of you are not going to be there after you go into combat." You have to be able to defend yourself in combat. They teach you how to do hand-to-hand combat, and how to kick. The last thing you want to do is use your hands. Use rocks, a chair, a knife, anything goes when you are in a fight with the enemy.

When we went out for training you learn how to read a map and how to evade the enemy. If they catch you, they can dunk you in water and beat on you. All you are supposed to give the enemy is your name, rank and serial number. You can't tell them how many men you are with, or what company, regiment or battalion you are in.

We would simulate being captured at night in the woods and they let us escape. They would go after us and try to catch us. If they caught us, they would beat on us. If there was more of us than them, we would fight them, we wouldn't let them take us as prisoners. A lot of times we would just outrun them. We learned how to stay warm by using the buddy system. We would lie next to one another to generate heat so we wouldn't freeze to death.

While in AIT we learned about our weapons and how to evade the enemy, reading maps, and going out at nighttime. In the morning we were up doing PT. After an hour of exercising the sergeant would yell, "What do you want," we would yell back, **"More PT sergeant."** Then we would do more jumping jacks, pushups, and sit-ups. Then we would go back in to clean our barracks and make our beds, then have breakfast.

****

I would like to preface some of the upcoming stories with some historical context. I am describing the events as they occurred from the perspective of what was happening in the 1960s. The stories reflect the times and location, which include a very controversial war in a very controversial time. I take responsibility for the language choices I use here, as I am adding them in for context.

Buffing the Floor

One time I had to buff the floors, we had three days left in AIT. A tall, black guy came in, who I didn't know, runs across the floor, and I yell, "Get off the floor," he yells something back to me, and he runs back across the floor again. I said, "Go around, I am buffing the floor." I said again, "Just get off the floor, you idiot." He stops and comes back. (I saw him the week before punch another dark-skinned soldier in the mouth, who he was arguing with.) He came towards me like he was going to punch me and said "Are you talking to me?" Then, I just punched him in the mouth. I dropped him and he hit the floor. Just then they called revelry and he didn't get up. I walked outside and I stopped on the steps, I should have just gone down the steps. Apparently, he got up and grabbed the broom handle and hit me on the back of the head. He broke the broom handle. I fell down and I got back up. I was drowsy. Everyone heard it crack. They grabbed him and put me in a Jeep and took me to the hospital where they X-rayed my head. I was okay, nothing was fractured. I must have a hard head. When I returned to the barracks the sergeant said the captain wants to see you up in his office. This guy was there, his name was Dawson, he was from Philadelphia, PA, same as me. The captain said the situation was racial. I said, "It was not racial." The captain said, "This is 1965, I am not going to have any racial problems here." I tried to tell the captain my side of the story but he didn't want to hear it. So, we both got an Article 15 and they took our rank away from us.

A little side note: After I went to jump school and Vietnam, I got out of the service and I was in Philly waiting for my friend Jimmy Canty to pick up his pay check on Susquehanna & Allegheny Aves. I was standing outside leaning on his car when two guys came walking by, and I recognized them as Dawson with his friend. He walked by me and he stops and talked to his friend. His friend looked back at me and smiled. Then they both started walking back towards me. I got off the car and stood in a defensive stance. He stopped about four feet from me and he asks, "Were you in the service?" I said, "Yes." He said, "Is your name Cubbage?" I said, "Yes." "Do you know who I am?" I said, "Yes, you are Dawson." "You aren't mad at me, are you?" I said "No." He came a couple of steps closer and shook my hand. He said, "Did you go to Vietnam?" I said "Yes." Dawson said, "I went to Germany. I heard that a lot of guys we trained with got killed over there." I said "Yes, they did." He said, "I got busted in Germany." I said, "I got busted in Vietnam." We both laughed.

My friend Jimmy Canty came out and he didn't know what was going on. He stood behind them and he didn't say a word. I said, "This is my friend, Jimmy." They said, "Hi" to him. We shook hands, we left pretty friendly; I didn't take anything personal, if he wanted to be friends, now, it was okay by me. He knew I wouldn't take any stuff from him, and without a stick he wouldn't be able to beat me. I never saw Dawson again. I don't know if this story is interesting or not, but I like telling it.

Airborne Training, Fort Benning, Georgia, December, 1965

Two days later, I left Fort Gordon, Georgia and I went to Fort Benning, Georgia for Airborne Training.

It was Christmas time and we spent a week running around yelling "Airborne" and doing pushups. We had to do double time everything, twice as fast, do more pushups, do PLF (Parachute, Land & Fall). We had different training: jumping off two-foot logs, and stands, how to roll, and slide down 35-foot towers and 250-foot towers. They would bring you all the way up with a parachute on, let you go, and then they would teach you how to fall. Sergeants would yell at you with loud speakers, "Keep your legs bent, look over the horizon, close your eyes so it won't shock you, you don't' want to get scared, don't look down, don't stiffen up because that will break your legs."

It was Christmas time and they gave us four days off. The airlines had military standby tickets that were half price. If the plane was fill, they would put you on the next plane. In 1965 the planes were hardly ever filled. They would not feed you until everyone else was fed and got their meals. The stewardesses would say, "You didn't pay full price, if we don't have enough, you don't get any food." If they had extra, they would feed you. It was another way of them disrespecting the military. You never hear about that. It happened every time I flew *military stand-by*.

Happy New Year, 1966 with my Buddy, The Fogue Guy

After Christmas leave, I went back to Fort Benning, Georgia and I continued my training.

My buddy, Jimmy Fogarty, was nearby in basic training at Fort Gordon. It was New Year's Eve and I got an overnight pass. I jumped on the bus for $2.

I went and saw him. I said, "Let's go to Atlanta, GA and celebrate New Year's Eve, 1966." He said he was only in Basic Training for two weeks and he didn't have leave. He went back to his barracks anyway, and he got dressed. He put his helmet and two gloves in the bed to make it look like he was sleeping. One of the soldiers in his barracks said, "Hey, you are going to be AWOL." I said to him," We will be back in a few hours, we are just going out for a few drinks. Don't say anything to anyone." He said, "Ok, I won't."

We flagged down a cab and we told him to take us to Atlanta. The MPs stopped us at the gate and we thought, oh, no… they were going to ask us for our passes. But they didn't, they told the driver, "One of your headlights are out, don't come back until you get that fixed."

We had a nice time in the bars and we welcomed in the New Year, 1966. By now, we were drunk, and we decided to go back to Jimmy's barracks at base camp. This time we made sure we stopped a cab that had two headlights. We went back to his barracks; I had no place to sleep. There were a couple of empty bunks, so I laid down on an empty bunk at about 2:00 in the morning and went to sleep. At 5:30 am in comes Jimmy's sergeant yelling at everybody, "Get up, we are going to have a Happy New Year, as soon as we start running." He saw me and he realized I didn't belong there after he sees my uniform. My uniform is just plain, no medals, yet. He yelled, "What the f... are you doing here?" "I don't know, I was out drinking, and I decided to come in here and go to sleep. I got the barracks mixed up." He yelled, "Get out of my f... barracks now!" As I got up to leave, he followed me outside, yelling, "Get out of my barracks." He said outside, "Hey soldier, where are you from? "I am from Fort Benning; I am a paratrooper." He said, "Ahh, a paratrooper." Then he started talking really nice to me. He said, "Go up to the mess hall, for a dollar you can get a nice breakfast." I said, "thank you." He said, "just stay out of my barracks." I said "No problem." The sergeant went back into the barracks yelling at the soldiers to get dressed. I started laughing, thinking about my friend Fogue and what he will be doing for the next couple of hours with a hangover.

I went up to the mess hall and I said to the cook, "The sergeant said for $1.00 I can eat here." The cook said, "You're in the army, right?" I said, "Yeah, "I am from Fort Benning." He said, "I don't care where you are from, you're in the army, aren't you?

You eat for nothing." I got my food and sat by the window.

Twenty minutes later I saw Jimmy running by with his company singing cadence. I had to laugh. About an hour later they came running by again. Two hours later, he came into the mess hall. I was still sitting there, and we started having breakfast together. Fogue said he threw up a couple of times while he was running. I just laughed. I said, "We Had a good time last night, didn't we?" He said "Yea." I said, "I have to go back to training. See you later."

Afterwards, I met my best friend, The Fogue Guy, a couple of times, while we were both in Vietnam. I'll tell you that story later…

Back to Fort Benning, GA., Airborne Training

I took a bus back to Fort Benning for $1.50. It was cheaper going back, why? We don't know why. Everyone used to say, "That's the army for you."

The next day we were back training: running, jumping off of logs, and three-foot stools. We would run with our parachutes on our backs for hours. It would seem like my heart would come out of my chest. I met good friends in training. They would help me finish the training for the day.

We started jumping out of C130 planes on last five days of jump school. After you put on your parachute, they would check it, and double check it, before you went up in the plane.

One guy got into the plane and something made his parachute open up and it smashed him all around the plane and it pulled him out of the plane. He died. They stopped jumping for two days, while they did an investigation. They had to find out the reason his shoot opened inside the plane. Then we started jumping again.

I was the first man at the door the third time we jumped. The sergeant was yelling at me "Are you scared?" I yelled back, "Yes, sergeant." He said "Look over the horizon, don't look down, I am going to kick you in the ass and you are not even going to feel it. Do you hear what I said?" I said, "Yes, sergeant." All of a sudden, I am out the door of the plane, I am counting 1,000, 1001,1002,1003, and the shoot opened up. The sergeant was right, I never felt his kick.

We went to the beer garden that night and all the guys would talk about how exciting it was jumping from C130 planes and laughing about things that happened that day. Everyone had an exciting story to tell. Sharing and listening to experiences with friends in the beer garden and in the barracks was one of my favorite memories of jump school.

One experience I had was when I landed on a parachute. The guy yelled at me to get off his parachute. I said, "I am trying," They taught us in jump school if you don't get off that parachute your chute will collapse because you do not have any weight pulling on the chute.

I tried to run off of it. It was like running on a cloud. I kept on sinking into the chute, but I finally scrambled off.

After you get five jumps in, you become a paratrooper. They have a ceremony and they pin you. It's the next step above being a regular soldier or a leg. Then you could become an air-borne ranger or you can become a green beret, if you want to. A green beret and an air-borne ranger have a longer training time and you have to stay in the army longer than two years. A paratrooper was good enough for me. I got $55 more a month for being a paratrooper.

Before I was drafted, I met my friend, Tommy Powers. He told me about jumping out of planes and I could get $55 more a month for doing that.

That's why I joined. I got paid $65 a month for being a private, and $55 for being a paratrooper. I made $120 a month or $30 a week.

In class they gave you the history of paratroopers jumping out of planes in World War II. They jumped from too high an altitude, 18,000 or 20,000 feet on D-Day. It took them twenty minutes to reach the ground. It gave the enemy enough time to shoot them while in the air. About 40% of paratroopers were killed on D-Day because the enemy had plenty of time to shoot them down. They were too high up, and they spent too much time in the air.

Now, they slide down from helicopters on ropes that are only 100 feet from the ground. They are ready to fight in seconds, once they land.

The Airborne combat jumps are between 600 and 800 feet. The training jumps are 1400 feet and it takes you about four minutes to get down to the ground.

When you jump out of a plane, you count, 1000, 1001, 1002, 1003. If you don't feel a pull on your shoulder, if the chute doesn't open up, then you pull your reserve in the front of you. Guys would say "Sergeant, what happens if the chute doesn't work?"

He said, "Bring it back, we'll give you a new one." "Sergeant, what happens if they both don't work?" He would say, "Bring them both back and we'll give you two new ones." It was funny at the time, and everyone would laugh, it was a big joke. The sergeants would always begin the class with a paratrooper joke. I don't remember them now, but at the time they were funny.

My Going Away Party

After graduating from jump school, I got a ten day leave to go home to Philly. My friend, Ed Collins said he was going to have a going away party for me. Jimmy Fogarty, the Fogue Guy, was on his way to supply school in Missouri and I invited him to the party too. During the party Fogue asked me. "Why are you becoming a paratrooper?" I answered, "Fogue, don't worry about it, you could never make it, as a paratrooper," and I walked away from him. I knew that comment would get his goat. About ten minutes later he came over to me and said, "As soon as I get back to Fort Leonard Wood, Missouri, I am going to join up for Airborne School" and he did!

Three girls briefly came to the party, Jimmy's girlfriend at the time, Janet Smith, Gloria Grant and another girl, who we never met before, Elaine

Hennessy, a pretty little blonde. She wouldn't even give me the time of day. Five years later on Sunday, July 20, 1969, the day Neil Armstrong landed on the moon, I met Elaine Hennessy again at the Gables in Margate, New Jersey. We were married two years later, July 10, 1971. Meeting Elaine again, was the best thing that ever happened to me!

Janet Smith sent the Fogue guy a Dear John letter when he first went to Vietnam, and my girlfriend, Maryanne Kline, sent me a Dear John letter too, when I first went to Vietnam. They told us that 75% of the soldiers will receive a Dear John letter and they were right.

When I flew to California, on my way to Vietnam, I met up with a lot of guys I trained with in jump school and AIT.

Friends as Close as Brothers

I had a good friend who helped me and trained with me in jump school, his name was **Pfc Richard Recupero**, a little skinny guy, from PepsiCo, Florida. He got married as soon as he graduated high school. He didn't have a job so he joined the service. He was a RA (regular army). I had a lot of good friends in the service. **Pfc Thomas Vontor** was from Philadelphia and **Tom Bommarito** was from Detroit. Tom and I are still good friends today. When I got into the incident with Dawson, Bommarito was outside and he saw him hit me with the broom handle when it broke over my head. He was one of the guys who hung around with me in jump school. He said, "I always looked up to you, Cubby, because I always thought you were a tough guy." I told him, "I am not a tough guy, I just have a hard head." Other good friends I made were: Andersen, Holyfield, Woodhouse, and Underwood. Woodhouse helped me a lot in jump school and AIT.

Woodhouse and I, in AIT and Airborne Training

Woodhouse and I would clean our weapons together, polish our boots, run, jog, and talk to one another. When I was really tired of running with 50 pounds of equipment on my back, he would stop and wait with me until I got my breath. He would have 50 pounds on his back, too. They would say, "You don't have to finish first, just as long as you finish, don't quit." Sometimes I would think, "I can't take it." Those guys would stop you from dropping out, saying "Come on, you can do it, just hang in there."

In the service you are as close as a brother to one another. There's a strong bond there. They help you accomplish different things in the service; you need them.

Woodhouse and I, in Vietnam

Another fond memory of Woodhouse was whenever we would come across each other in Vietnam, he would tell me how many days we had left in Vietnam, 212, next time, 206. Every time I saw him, he would give me a countdown.

Once, his platoon was in a firefight and a bullet went through a tree, then it went through his helmet. His helmet had a hole in it. He showed me, and we laughed about it. He asked me if he could use my helmet to shave because his helmet had a hole in it. They wanted him to turn his helmet in for a new one and he said, "No way, I am taking this home with me."

Once, we went 24 days without shaving and showering, while we were out in the field. Woodhouse looked at me and I looked at him and he said, "Cubbage, is that you?" and I said,

"Woodhouse, is that you?" and we just laughed. It was the longest time I ever went without shaving and showering.

Another time, I saw Woodhouse, he was minesweeping a road. I said "Hey," he said, "I am mine sweeping a road. I like this job. They needed someone and I just volunteered for it."

About a week later he was back in my company again. I ran into him at the mess hall. He said, "I got put back into my platoon because I swept a road and a f... jeep came down the road, that I just swept, and the f... jeep got blown up. So, they put me back here again."

I said, "Welcome back, my man."

A month later our company got into another firefight and word came down that Woodhouse was one of three guys that 'bought the farm.' I was heartbroken for a long time; another friend was gone. There was a saying that went around the camp: "Better him than me." I never liked that saying. Sometimes soldiers were wounded and they were shipped to Japan and we would hear that they were killed without knowing for sure. Woodhouse is not on the wall so he is probably alive. I have been trying to track him down ever since I got out of Vietnam.

Bell's Ominous Premonition, February, 1966

On my way over to California from Philadelphia I sat next to a guy named, Bell. We went to AIT and Jump School together. We knew one another, we were friends, but we didn't hang out together We sat next to each other on the plane. He said to me, "Cubbage, I am going to be killed by Easter. I just have a feeling." I said, "No, what are you talking about, no, no way, we don't know what we are going into." We talked for a while. He was from Southwest Philadelphia and I told him I was from Swampoodle. He knew it was in North Philadelphia. We had a nice time talking. We were both supposed to go to the 173rd Airborne Brigade.

In the middle of March, while we were in the jungle, one of the guys came up to me and said, "Did you know Bell? He was from Philadelphia and you went to jump school together. "Well, he bought the farm." or "He got waxed." I never liked either one of those expressions but I guess it was better than saying he was killed.

Some guys stayed in touch with each other after training at AIT and Jump School by writing back and forth. That's how they knew what happened to different guys in other outfits.

That was in March, I don't remember the exact date but it was before Easter. When I came home, I never tried to contact his parents. They lived in southwest Philly.

There were a lot of guys I wish I had contacted their parents when I got home. That's one of the regrets I have.

Hawaii, February 21, 1966

We left from Oakland, California, then we had a layover in Hawaii for eight hours. We decided to go into Oahu to have a few drinks and see what Hawaii looked like. We went into different bars and had fun. We went into one bar and Don Ho was singing. When we got in there, they gave us a red coin to have one free drink, because we were in uniform. Don Ho came out and sang songs and told some jokes. He told all the servicemen the first drink was on him. Don Ho said he was in the air force in the Korean War. He became a pilot. He received his pilot's license the day the Korean War ended. He laughed and said, "They knew I was coming over so that's why they ended the war." He seemed like a great guy.

We left his club and while walking down the street we ran into a friend of mine, Howie, from New York. They said we looked like brothers. He told us he went in to have his palm read for $2 and he gave the lady a $20 bill. The lady left the room, never read his palm, then, a big man came in and said, you have to leave. He said, "I am waiting for my change." He said, "There is no one here, you have to leave."

I said, "Let's go back, I'll get your money for you." So about five of us went back. He showed me the house on the street and I banged on the door. A big, heavy Hawaiian guy came out and said there is no one here, come back tomorrow. I said we can't come back tomorrow; we want our money now. He said come back tomorrow. I punched him, then he punched me, I fell to the ground. My friends were all cheering and yelling, "Come on Cubbage, get up," and I got up to punch him again, and he punched me right in my face. I fell back about four or five feet, a car came and slammed on his brakes, he almost hit me. I got up and I knew I was not going to beat him. I said, "I'm going back to base camp." We flagged a cab down and we went back to Scofield barracks.

I went to sleep and got up the next morning. I walked over to the latrine and looked into the mirror, one eye was closed and all blackened. I just laughed and said, "Oh man, did I mess up." I washed up and went over to the mess hall. Everyone was saying. "It looks like you have already been in a war. Do you know you could be court-marshalled for damaging government property"? I found out that the guy I fought was one of those big Samoans you hear about.

This was the beginning of a bad year…
Camp Alpha, Vietnam, February 22, 1966

I got on a plane in Hawaii and we flew to Vietnam, it was about a twelve-hour flight. We landed in Camp Alpha. We were there for about three days.

On the second day, they picked me and four other soldiers out, for a detail. They gave us a M14 rifle and a magazine with one bullet in it. We walked down the road and a Spec 4 was there. He said you guys have a real good job if you want it. It will attract a lot of kids. They might have a grenade on them, so keep them off. Just shoot up in the air and they will run away. We are going to dump the garbage out into a big hole. We pulled up to the hole and about 600 kids, ages 7 – 14 years old, came running over and started climbing up onto the truck to eat the garbage. They were starving. It was the saddest sight

I ever saw. We started dumping it into the pit and the kids jumped into the pit, and started eating it. The Spec 4 came running back, yelling, and he started throwing sand and dirt on top of the garbage, that stopped the kids from eating it. He started yelling at us. He yelled at us and said we did not move fast enough to get rid of the garbage. The sand stopped the kids from grabbing the food and eating it. We didn't know all of this was going to happen. He got cocky with us and said, this was a good job and he could have kept us here, and we wouldn't have to go out into the jungles and get killed. We started arguing with him and all four of us told him what we thought of him and called him names. We said to him, "Go f… yourself, you j-o." We were glad to get back to camp.

At Camp Alpha they played music all day long. Every other song was 'The Green Beret'. They would call about 50 names an hour to go up to headquarters to get your assignment. I was supposed to go to 173rd Airborne, but when my name was called and I went up, they told us we were all going to the '1st Infantry Division, the Big Red One'. About 50 of my friends who graduated from AIT and Jump School with me, started hollering, "We are paratroopers, we're not legs. We want to go into an airborne outfit that we were assigned to." The Sgt hollered back, "Just shut the f… up, you are going into the Big Red One. You are going to get your jump pay, you are going to get your regular pay, and you are going to get your hazardous duty or combat pay which is $65 more a month. We made $65 regular army pay, $55 jump pay, $65 for hazardous/combat pay and $10 for being overseas for a total of $195 a month, all tax free because we were overseas. I kept about $50 and I sent the rest of my money home.

They yelled, "Has everybody signed their insurance policy? We would feel bad if your parents got cheated out of $10,000 because you didn't sign your insurance papers? Now, get on that f**king truck."

Phuoc Vinh, Vietnam, February 26, 1966

They drove us to our base camp, Phuoc Vinh. We went down to our supply sergeant and they gave us a rifle, M16, two clips, and about 120 rounds of ammunition, a poncho liner, a backpack, a trench shovel and other equipment. We went back up to our tents and we met our sergeant, Sergeant Lewis J. Jackson. He was an E6, from North Carolina. He was a good guy. He said, "When we go out, we have to watch what we do, we have to make sure we all come back alive. We are in an area where the enemy would like to kill us."

Guys We Met in Our Tent

Some of the guys, from the 1st Infantry, came over on a boat, three months before we got there. They would not talk to us because they said, they didn't want to feel bad if we got killed. They had already been in combat and saw some of their friends get killed. Those guys in our tent were leaving in a few months, and they didn't want to get to know us. We were replacing the soldiers that got wounded or killed. They told us their Captain Costello was killed about three weeks before we got there,

I said "Hi, I'm Ed Cubbage," they said, "I don't care what your name is, if I get friendly with you, I'll feel bad if you get shot and killed" I said, "Hey, what makes you think I'll be shot before you, you moron." It caused a lot of hard feelings in the beginning. Then they came around and we eventually became friends, once we let them know we were paratroopers and we weren't going to take any bullshit from any of them, then things changed.

TK Stone came over on the ship with them, but he was friendly from the beginning. He tells the story when the 1st Infantry came over, the 173rd was there waiting for them. The 173rd teased them, "You guys are going to stay here, get all shot up, get killed, and we are going back to Guam or the United States. However, a few days later they found out they were being sent up to the Highlands. (the mountains in Vietnam) that was just as bad, if not worse, than where they were. The 1st infantry teased them, saying, "Goodbye, have fun up there, shoot straight."

Building Bunkers

The next day we started filling up sand bags. They brought in combat engineers with heavy equipment and we started building big bunkers, probably 20 feet long and 20 feet wide. It was pretty big. The heavy equipment would dig a four-foot hole deep in the ground. We had to make sure the ground was flat for easy walking. All day long we would fill the sand bags up with dirt. Outside the hole we would stack three bags across then five bags high. Long steel sheets were used for the roof. Then we would put sand bags on top of the roof. It was very sturdy. We made sure we had a square window where we could shoot out from. It was pretty neat how we built them. We started bringing down water, sea rations, chairs and bunks. It was our home away from home.

Swimming

One of the first times we were out on patrol, in the middle of March, we were roaming around sweeping the area. We came by a river, and everyone asked, "Can we go swimming"? Sergeant Jackson, a pretty good guy, said, "Alright, I'll let you go swimming, I'll go back up and make sure there are no Viet Cong around." Tahike and TK Stone and four other guys were there with me. We took our clothes off; some went in nude, but a few of us kept our boxer shorts on. I was the new guy in the group.

Tahike yelled for help. I was next to him. He was holding up this guy named Adam. Adam was pulling him under and fighting with him. I swam over to them and I yelled, "Calm down now, Adam, I got you." He completely pushed me under the water. Tahike swam away from him because Adam was drowning him. Adam was holding me under the water, then I pushed away from him, I had to come up for some air. Tahike swam back over to me and asked, where is he? I said, "We both were under the water, I had to break away from him, he was dragging me under the water, he was panicking, he never came back up again. I don't know what happened to him." Tahike started going down looking for him, and I tried too. We never found him.

When Sergeant Jackson came back, we told him what happened and then we got dressed. The captain brought the whole company down to search for him. Another platoon, not our platoon, found him a half-mile down the river. Sergeant Jackson said, "I will probably get in trouble for letting you guys go swimming. I have to go see Captain Lupus and tell him what happened." I said, "I will go down with you." He said, "No, I'll talk to the captain, he's new, he doesn't know me, I'll talk to him by myself." He came back and said the captain is not going to do anything to him. I put Tahike and you in for a commendation. The captain said only one commendation, "Cubbage is new, like me, he will have plenty of time to get commendations. We're not here for commendations or medals we are here to kill the VC. We'll just give the commendation to Tahike."

I said, "That's fine." I didn't know what a commendation was, at that time.

Operation Junction City

In March, 1966 we went out on an Operation called "Junction City." It was an 82-day military operation. We spent two weeks in the jungle, came back into base camp to get shaved, showered, get new fatigues and eat. Then we went back out to "Operation Junction City." As a result of this operation the VC moved most of their main force units across the border into Cambodia, rather than stationing them in South Vietnam where they were more vulnerable to attacks. The border sanctuaries in Cambodia were now expanded dramatically, creating further tension between Cambodia and South Vietnam and its Allies.

The land was a dangerous enemy by itself, but the biggest threat was the dangers it concealed. Whether in the thick of the jungle or deep in the rice paddies, the landscape was strange to us, but it was familiar to the VC, who expertly hid themselves in the land. We had vastly superior firepower, we had the upper hand, face to face, but the VC deliberately avoided large-scale conflicts where they could be outgunned. An area could be cleared of Viet Cong in the morning, but be back in enemy hands at sundown, after our troops had departed.

Instead, they waited in the vegetation for nightfall. They hid landmines and booby traps to inflict casualties and heighten the fear that we all felt with every step. We fought back with bombing campaigns that sprayed napalm that burned the skin off soldiers and civilians alike.

We used Agent Orange to raze the tropical foliage, destroying the trees and bushes. Sgt. Jackson broke a leaf off a branch and ate it, he said, "This is not going to hurt you but it will kill all the vegetation, so we can see the enemy.

They stopped using Agent Orange in 1971. The number of Vietnam Veterans affected by the chemical Agent Orange is astonishing. Roughly 300 thousand veterans have died from Agent Orange exposure, that's almost five times as many as the 58 thousand who died in combat. Often, we could see the helicopters spraying agent orange above us and thought nothing of it.

Operation Birmingham

During April and May, 1966, the 1st Battalion, 2nd Infantry played a key role in one of the most successful missions of destruction of the war. The operation, conducted in the Tay Ninh Province, some 70 miles northwest of Saigon, was called "Operation Birmingham." We were on a "search and destroy" mission. We cut off a major Viet Cong supply route from Cambodia into War Zone "C," a Viet Cong secret zone which had gone unchallenged for years.

Attacking north for four days through a continuous chain of camps and supply areas, the "Ramrods," our nickname, seized, destroyed and burned with gasoline more than 500 tons of rice, 100 tons of salt and 400 gallons of cooking oil, along with numerous military items and several dozen base camps.

On April 30, near the Village of Lo Go, we came under heavy machine gun and small arms fire from the Cambodian side of the river. Word came down to us saying they don't want us shooting across the border. They started shooting at us first; we shot back. We were the first American soldiers to fire across the Cambodian border. The VC knew we weren't supposed to fire across the border into Cambodia, so they would run there for sanctuary.

On May 31st a similar operation netted three Viet Cong and sunk two escaping sampans at Phuoc Hoa, a village six miles south of Phuoc Vinh. Such operations proved the skill and precision of our battalion in moving at night, and it taught the Viet Cong that darkness does not always offer sanctuary from the skill of the 'Ramrod' Infantrymen.

The enemy fought in typical guerrilla fashion, attacking the armored task force with mortars, recoilless rifles, automatic and small arms from prepared positions on both sides of the road. The American forces counter-attacked with every available weapon, including flame throwers and cannister shells to repel the fierce attacks.

Throughout May, June and July the 1st Battalion was used as the fire brigade of the 'Big Red One' Division. On four separate occasions we were deployed to distant areas on one-hour notice or less. These moves were made in counter action to Viet Cong operations during the 'Monsoon Offensive' and were a severe test of our battalion's flexibility and stamina.

I remember when I was under fire, I had only two clips and 120 bullets. As I was being shot at, and trying to put the bullets into the clip, I dropped three out of the four bullets. After that, I knew I had to get more ammunition clips. A clip is a device that is used to store bullets, ready for insertion into a rifle.

By the time I left Vietnam I had 25 to 30 clips that I carried.

Shit Houses

April, 1966, the engineers built two wooden shit houses. Three seats for the officers, and four seats for the soldiers. Five-hundred-pound iron barrels were cut in two halves, and they were used for the waste in the shit houses. You would have to pull them out with a rope and you would assign people to put gasoline in it and burn it. The officers had their own shit house and the regular GIs had theirs. After you come back from being in the field, they would put you on that detail. There were other places where you would dig a hole and put pipes in them, and take a leak. There were about 20 of them, 5 feet apart from each other.

One time we were assigned to do the officers' shit house. There were two sets of barrels. You take one out and put gasoline in it, and burn it, then put the empty one back in. John Lloyd said, "Hey, why don't we put gasoline in one of them, and put it back, maybe those ass holes will set themselves on fire." Thomas Vontor and I said, "Fine, that's okay with us."

An officer came down to use the officer's shit house while we were still working on the soldier's shit house. We looked at one another and said "Oh shit, we should have waited until we were done, to put gasoline in one of the officer's barrels." But the officer came out, safe and sound, and went back up to his area. We quickly finished our job and left.

About two hours later, we were down in our bunker, and a big fire broke out in one of the shit houses. An officer threw a cigarette down in the barrel and a big fire broke out. Thank God no one got hurt or we may have gone to jail for that one. Different guys knew we did it. They couldn't prove that it was done deliberately. Then they made new rules. After we were finished cleaning the shit houses, we had to make sure it wasn't flammable by throwing a match down into the barrel to test it. I don't know how long that lasted. That was a funny incident. We were lucky we didn't get caught. The officers had to go without a shit house for a month. They had to use ours, they were not happy about that. I don't know if the officers ever knew we were the ones that did it, but we were never assigned to that detail again.

The EM Club

They opened up an EM Club (entertainment). A friend of mine, Pfc Richard Glenn, they call him the "Bird," a skinny black guy from City Line in Philly, was walking up to the EM Club. A couple of white guys walked up to him and punched him, and they kept on walking up to the club. Bird was really upset about them.

That night at the EM Club someone turned the light switch off and bullets were shot, while four black guys were singing and dancing on stage. Two of them were killed, and two were wounded. It was a big thing, everyone was upset. They shut everything down. The officers made us bring all our weapons up to the CP to be checked. We did not have our names on the rifles and they were not marked. They had serial numbers on them but we never kept track of them at the time. I only knew the last few numbers on my rifle...899. After this incident we put different patches on them to make it easier to identify our rifles. The officers checked to see if our weapon was fired recently, if it smelled of gunfire; it was recently used.

Two days later they caught two white guys who were from Alabama who did the shooting. One guy must have turned the other guy in. They were sentenced to twenty years or life in prison, I don't know for sure, they could still be in jail today. That caused a lot of tension for a while between the whites and blacks in base camp.

Colonel Richard Prillaman, read the riot act to us, when he called us all together. He said it was a racial attack, two white guys from Alabama shot four black guys, two died and two lived. The two white guys were going to jail for a long, long time, they might spend the rest of their lives in jail. Out in the field we all need one another; our lives depended on it.

When we went out into the jungle all the tension was gone. We're a team, there is no black and white out in the foxhole.

There were a lot of different incidences that happened in base camp, let alone out in the field.

Bird was upset about what happened to him. I said it could have been the same two guys who punched you. We didn't know. Bird and I were always friends. There were a few incidences that we were involved in with other soldiers. I'll tell you more about that later.

Another Operation

April, 1966, Sergeant Jackson said "We are going on a big operation tomorrow; we'll be flying on helicopters and landing with a lot of shooting around us. We have to make it over to the wood line or jungles, in an area as big as a football field. 'C' company will come over to help us, but we have to make it over to the wood line. We will catch the VC in an "L" shape. Shooting could be light or heavy, we don't know how many VC are there. You can do whatever you want tonight, you have a few hours to go down to the airfield. The chaplain will be down there. You can see him if you want to. They are going to have some beer and ice cream for you.

Pfc Richard Recupero

Pfc Richard Recupero came up all excited and said my wife just had a baby. He was pretty young, 17 or 18. He couldn't find a job so he joined the army. I went through jump school with him. He was one of the skinny guys that helped me get through AIT and Jump School.

He started telling me, "I am not going down to 'B' company to see you anymore; I am going to stay with my 'C' company." He said, "Pfc Thomas

Vontor is always threatening me with his 45." They always played cards together. Vontor told him, "If you keep winning, I am going to shoot you." I said "Na, that's a bunch of bullshit, he is not going to shoot you, he is a South Philly guy who just wants to scare you, I'll handle him, he won't bother you. He just wants to intimidate you." Recupero said, "Guys from 'C' Company want me to stay down there with them. They asked me why am I always going to 'B' Company?"

I said, "That's fine, you stay down there with them."

He told me he was thinking about staying in the army but he can't wait until he goes home to see his wife and baby.

I saw the chaplain and he gave me absolution. He said, "You don't have to tell me all your sins, one by one, I'll give you a general absolution. I can do other religions too, Jewish or Protestant, it doesn't matter what religion you are."

Then we went back up to our tent and Sergeant Jackson gave us c-rations for 5 or 6 days. They consisted of spaghetti and meatballs, beans and franks, ham and eggs, fruit cocktail, peaches which were delicious and a small pound cake. We all hated the ham and lima beans; they were the worse. It also contained four cigarettes, chewing gum, candy, instant coffee and some toilet paper. The date on them were 1944 and 1945. They were all leftover from World War II. Some of the guys would laugh and say, "Look, they made this food before I was even born." We put them in big, woolen, brown socks. We hung them outside our backpack. We then got ready for the next day.

We got up early the next morning and went down to the airfield. The helicopters came in to get us. Sergeant Jackson said, "You stick with me, Cubbage, make sure the guys don't fall behind, so they don't shoot us in the back." I got along well with Sergeant Jackson.

When we jumped off the helicopters, we ran over to the wood line. We started firing and there wasn't any return fire, no one was there. Then we heard firing coming from the other end of the field, where "C" company was. We came up the side of the jungle and helped "C" company. We were in an "L" shape, firing our weapons. Shortly afterwards I heard Pfc Richard Anthony Recupero, from Florida, died on April 24, 1966 in Kontum province, and two other soldiers were killed, along with eight VCs. My heart was broken again. I was just talking to him the night before.

Stand on Your Toes, LBJ

When my friend Little Bitty Johnson, "LBJ," from Pittsburg, got drafted they said he was too small to get into the army. He went back to the army doctor a second time and he told him, "All my friends are being drafted and I want to go into the army, too." The doctor told him to stand on his toes. Then he said, "You are tall enough now, you pass." About three months later he was killed in Vietnam.

We went to visit LBJ's friend (the tall guy in the picture standing next to

46

him) when we got out of the service. We stopped at his house and he told me a week before, he and his dad were out partying and drinking. On the way home he crashed his truck and his dad was killed. They buried him about two days before we got there. I hugged him and talked to him for a little bit then I said, "I'll see you later, sorry about your dad." Ed Collins and I left and waved goodbye. I'm sorry I lost his name and his phone number and I never saw him at any reunions.

Beer

May, 1966, we went out on ambush patrols and I hated going out at night. We would go to one position, move, and then onto another position. If the VC came down the path, we would open up and shoot.

We were in Vietnam for two weeks, when we started going out on ambush patrol. We had to do a road clearance for the trucks, by sweeping the road with metal detectors to make sure there were no bombs in the road.

The trucks were coming to resupply us, and a friend from our company, Johnson, we called him LBJ (little bitty Johnson from Pittsburg) had cases of beer in the back of the truck. When he saw us, he started dropping cases of beer onto the road. I grabbed a case and Sgt. Torres, a little cocky guy, grabbed a case of beer too. Then he started yelling to me, "That's my beer, bring that back to me. Come here private." I kept running and brought it back to my company. The other guys grabbed the cases of beer and brought them back to their own places. All the guys were happy and laughing while we were drinking the beer.

I was with the guys and a Spec 4, Tahika, a Hawaiian guy, T.K Stone and Thomas Vontor. Torres came over to me and said, "Didn't I tell you to bring the beer back?" I said, "It's not yours, that was my friend, Johnson, who dropped off the beer for us. He saw me, and that's why he dropped it off." Sgt, Torres took two cans and left, but he had a whole case back in his area.

A Thief in the Night

A few weeks later I was up at the bunker pulling guard duty when a friend of mine, Lou Rivera, from New York & Puerto Rico, came down and said, "Look, I have to go out on ambush patrol tonight and I won all this money in a card game, if something happens to me I don't want the Viet

Cong to end up with all this money. I want you to hold it for me, about $150." I said, "No problem."

When night came, I was outside the bunker sleeping. When you had guard duty you were awake two hours and then slept four hours. There were three of us who took turns, 2 hours on duty, and 4 hours off duty. When you were out in the field and in base camp someone had to be awake all the time. I fell asleep, and I had a memory that Torres, from Guam or Puerto Rico, woke me up and asked me a question. Then he said, "Go back to sleep." I had a slight memory that Torres took the money. When Rivera came back from ambush patrol, he asked for the money. I looked around and I said, "I don't have it." He wasn't too upset. I told him I think Torres stole the money. Rivera and I were friends, he knew I wouldn't take it.

About five days later Torres came up to me and said, "You keep telling everyone I stole your money. I ought to kick your ass." I said, "Try it." He kicked me in the groins. I went after him. I grabbed him and we hit the ground. I started punching him right in his face. My groins were really hurting, so I kept punching him; I was getting the best of him. Then Sergeant Jackson came up and pulled us apart. Torres got up and his nose and mouth were bleeding. Torres said, "I want him locked up and court marshalled for hitting and NCO." Sergeant Jackson said, "Oh no, you told me, down there, you were going to kick Cubbage's ass. I followed you up here, and I watched the whole thing. You started it, you got your ass kicked, and now you want him locked up. No, it doesn't work that way. Maybe some of the things he said were true about you, I don't know, who knows. You should have gone to the captain and reported it to the captain what Cubbage said about you." Torres walked away. Sergeant Jackson said, "Cubbage, you can't be fighting NCOs, you are going to get your ass in trouble one of these days." I said, "I know, I didn't start it." Sergeant Jackson said, "Maybe some of the things you said are true about Torres. He had a couple incidences in Oklahoma" (that's where they came from) ... then Sgt. Jackson just walked away.

Lou Rivera, a Good Friend

Shortly afterwards, my friend, Rivera, came up to me and said, "I heard you got into a big fight with Torres, I heard you really tuned him up." I said, "Yeah, he kicked me in my nuts, hard." Then Rivera said, "I told all my friends to go up to Torres and say, "Hey, I heard you stole money from Cubbage."

He never denied it, he just said that Cubbage was a f… liar. Torres got pissed that's why he came up looking for a fight. He had about five weeks left to go in the army. After the fight he went to see the captain and the captain let him leave two weeks early. One day he got into a jeep and they took him away. We never saw him again.

We just came back from the jungles; we were constantly walking in water. Most of it was more like thin mud, than it was water. Standing brackish water had leeches. The leeches in Vietnam were huge, reddish-black, slimy, blood-sucking globs. Leeches would find exposed skin like a magnet finds BBs. They get under shirts and into pants. There were two good ways to get them off. You could burn them with a cigarette or you could spray them with insect repellent. The cigarette trick was the fastest. Bug juice was the preferred method because it was plentiful and leeches hated it. A little squirt of it would make them curl up and fall off. Without a heavy application of it, the mosquitos would eat you alive at night. Bug juice was a tool of war. We used it for lighting fires, cleaning weapons, repelling creatures great and small.

After coming back from the jungles some of the guys noticed we had leeches on us. If one guy found a leech, we all had them. We used the buddy system to check the places that we couldn't see. I found three or four of them on me and I began burning them with my cigarette, and they fell right off. Other guys put mosquito repellent, or bug juice, on it and they would fall right off.

Lou Rivera fainted and fell down. The guys took off his shirt and they found about five leeches on his chest and stomach. Then they took off his pants and he had a big leech on his groins. It was gigantic! They poured mosquito repellant on it. They sent him off to the hospital and that was the first time he got malaria. Rivera and I remained good friends. He spent eight weeks in the hospital after he caught malaria.

After the second time he caught malaria, they sent him home. I heard he got married when he went home. I tried tracking Louis Rivera down, but I couldn't find him.

The Body Count

Another time we were out on an operation, there were dead VC bodies lying on the ground that were killed by our artillery and by our shootings. They wanted us to bring them over to the road so they could have a body count. Then Johnny Moore said, "I have a rope." He tied it around their feet and he dragged the bodies over to the road. Then he gave Vontor and me the rope and we put the rope around the VC legs and dragged them over to the road. The VC bodies were stiff because rigor mortis had already set in. I heard the captain yell, "Cubbage, what the f**k are you doing? That is against the Geneva Convention. You are not allowed to drag those bodies, pick them up and carry them over to the road. If the news media saw that, they would have a field day, and I would be replaced."

Then we picked them up and brought them over to the road. We thought the Geneva Convention was about prisoners of war. He was pissed at us for the remainder of time he was stationed there. We brought about eight bodies over to the road. It was one of the few times we made contact with the VC and no one got wounded or killed.

On Patrol in the Jungles

We encountered many incidences when we went out into the jungles. It was chaotic and terrifying, and you'd never knew where Viet Cong soldiers would be hiding. They used guerrilla tactics, ambushing troops and running away into the jungle, and for all you knew they could be hiding right under your feet in tunnels.

When we swept the area; we would get sniper fire; and anytime we made contact it seemed like we would always have someone who would get wounded or killed. Sometimes you wouldn't know who it was until you came in from the field, and back into your tent. Their bunks would be empty, and all their stuff would be gone. You would find out they got wounded or they would say, "He bought the farm," which meant he was killed. Sometimes they would say. "Better him than me." I never liked any of those sayings.

Point Man

A point man is a navigator who walks several yards out in front of everyone else and is likely to be the first one to encounter enemy soldiers. It is a hazardous position that requires alertness and an ability to deal with unexpected attacks.

In June, 1966, I was the point man. I was cutting a path through the jungle and Pfc Charles E. Clark calls to me, "Cubbage, I am going to take your place now." Clark was a young skinny guy from Kansas City. We used to say to him, "Clark, you are not in

Kansas City anymore" …just like Dorothy in the Wizard of Oz. He told us the night before, that his mother wrote to him, and said she was worried about his sister because she just started protesting the Vietnam War.

It wasn't even five minutes, when Clark started pulling point. I just sat down to light up a cigarette and one shot was fired and someone yelled, "Sniper"! I was sitting on my helmet, I rolled off of it, and I started shooting up at the trees and into the air. Someone said, "Clark got hit." He was shot in his stomach. We looked all around and couldn't find the sniper; he went down into a tunnel. We couldn't find the tunnel. At times when we could find the tunnel, we would throw grenades down or shoot our rifles, down into the tunnel. If the sniper shot five minutes before, it would have been me, instead of Clark. Things changed in a second in Vietnam; one second someone would be screaming or yelling, the next second someone would be wounded or dead.

One time we found a tunnel that a sniper had escaped to and closed up. We threw a claymore mine into it and we set it off. It blew the door off and we could see a dead VC inside there.

Beer Cans, Flip Flops and Cool Aid

We had footlockers that you could buy from the Vietnamese or Gooks, (as they were sometimes called). They were made out of beer cans. They would glue or staple them together. We would put our clothes or boots inside them.

In Phuoc Vinh the walls of some of the buildings were made of aluminum beer cans. They would cut the beer cans, stretch them out, then staple or glue them together and make walls with them; it shows you how much beer and soda we drank in Vietnam.

The Vietnamese would take tires from old cars and trucks and make flip flops with them. They would attach string to them and wear the flip flips or sell them to the soldiers. Sometimes in the jungle you could see their footprints with the tire marks on them.

When we had mail call the guys would share their goodies with you: candy, cake and different flavors of cool aid like: root beer, strawberry, cherry, grape, lemon, and orange. It really tasted good with whiskey and vodka. It was funny some of the stuff we could make with it.

On Patrol

Then we started to go out in helicopters on patrol. We would ride for half an hour or more, then they would drop us off, and we would sweep the area. We had to jump off quickly, on hard ground or in the rice paddies. Sometimes the VC would be waiting for us; there were snipers, and little ambushes, not big fights, then the VC would escape back into the jungle. They climbed down into their tunnels under the ground. If we found the tunnel, we would put C4s in the tunnel and blow it up. Every time we made contact with the VC someone always got wounded or bought the farm.

When we went back into base camp, one guy shot himself in the foot, so he wouldn't have to go back out into the field again. He didn't come over with us on the plane, he came over with the ship.

I remember one time, another guy in our tent ran outside and he started shooting up at our planes. Then he went outside our perimeter. The captain called us up to the road, he wanted us to go out and get him with our weapons. We said, "No, we are not going out to get him, he's going to start shooting at us." Sergeant Jackson said, "He is either going to kill us, or we will have to kill him. We'll wait until he comes back, he will get hungry and thirsty sooner or later." The captain agreed. He came back about five hours later, he had his hands up, and they took his rifle away. They brought him down to our bunker and they said watch him until tomorrow, they are going to take him away.

He said to me, "Yo, Cub, I am okay, but when I go down and get interviewed tomorrow, I am going to beat the shit out of the officer, I don't care if he's a captain or not, the higher the rank the better it will be. I'm getting the F...out of here. I don't want to get killed." We talked for a while and then I said to him, "You do what you want to do. I am not going to say anything to anybody."

The next day the MPs came down and they took him away. We went out on patrol for two or three days.

When we came back all his stuff was gone. I said to someone in the CP, "Hey, what happen to him?" They said, "He's getting thrown out of the service on a section 8," (that meant you were crazy). He was interviewed by a major and all at once he started beating the hell out of the major. They had to call people in to pull him off; I laughed. Now they have MPs sitting in the room with the psychologists and soldier. I never heard about him again, he was from New York. Different things like that would happen.

Sergeant Lewis Jackson

A few weeks later, we flew in a helicopter again, and went out on patrol. Out of the 365 days I was in Vietnam, I was out in the field at least 330 days, or close to it. We started getting sniper fire. Shooting was all around us. Sergeant Jackson went behind an ant hill, when he looked up, he got hit right between the eyes. I didn't see it, afterwards, I just saw the back of his head.

Johnny Moore, the radio operator, started yelling, "Pull back, pull back." We all pulled back sixty feet or so. I said. "Sergeant Jackson is back there." A couple of guys said we have to get out of here before we all get killed. I said, "We can't leave him, we have to go back for him." A couple of the guys said there is nothing we can do, let's get the f...out of here. I said, "We can't leave him, he wouldn't leave us." After a few words were exchanged, I told them my plan. Let's load our rifles, and run back yelling and shooting. I told some guys to shoot at the trees and some to shoot down towards the ground. We reloaded our rifles and we ran back yelling and screaming. We pulled him out and then carried him to the landing zone. Johnny Moore got on the radio and asked for a helicopter to pick up Sergeant Jackson and our squad. About twenty minutes later two helicopters came down. We put him into the helicopter and returned to base camp.

Captain Lupus said to us, "Good job for bringing Sergeant Jackson back." I was really shocked that Sgt Jackson got killed. He was probably the best sergeant I ever had. I got along with him very well. I felt bad for a long time when this happened to him. Staff Sergeant Lewis James Jackson died on June 26, 1966, in Quang Tri province. He was from Missouri, married a girl from Germany.

Pfc Thomas Vontor, Pfc William Richard, Pfc Vernon Hollifield (we went to jump school together) Pfc Johnnie Moore, and Pfc James Brown were with us the day Sergeant Jackson got killed

Before Sergeant Jackson got killed the captain called us over and said, "We have to go up and help some guys who got into trouble." Sergeant Richardson was leading us and he said hold on to the person's backpack in front of you because it was so dark that night. We walked through streams and up hills. He marked the trees with his machete, so we could find our way back. Two hours later we found the bodies of four recon soldiers. We had two stretchers with us. They put two bodies on the stretchers, and the other two we put on our stretched-out ponchos. Four of us carried one, big, heavy guy on a poncho, which was hard to grasp onto. We had to carry them back through the streams and up the hills to our base camp in the pitch-black darkness. We got back to base camp around 2:00 am. We put the bodies on a truck. I don't know who they were, and I never heard anything about them afterwards. Sgt Richardson was in my company; he wasn't in my platoon. I knew him and he knew me. We became good friends when we started going to the "Big Red One Reunions"

MPs and an Article 15

Vontor and I just came back from being out in the boonies for about ten or fifteen days. We were in our base camp in Phuoc Vinh in our tent and it was before noon, Vontor says, "Let's sneak into town and see some mamasans and have a few drinks. We can be back in a few hours. We needed a drink. The captain is probably still pissed at us for dragging those gooks on the ground for a body count, instead of carrying them to the road." I said, "Okay." We went into town and we were drinking and having fun. We decided to go back to our base camp. We started walking to leave town, when two jeeps pulled up, two MPs in each jeep. They pulled in front of us. Vontor looked at me and said, "Hey, look Ed, they are going to give us a ride back to base camp. This is great." He ran over and climbed into the back of the jeep. The MPs jumped out, grabbed Vontor, who was half-way into the jeep, pulled him out of the jeep and threw him on the ground. I yelled at them, "What the f**k is going on? We are not doing anything." The MP said, "He was climbing into my jeep." I yelled at him, "We thought you were going to take us back to base camp." He turned around to me and said, "Do you know who I am, I am Miller, M I L E R, he spelled out his named. I laughed at him, then he smacked me in my face. I punched him, and the other two MPs grabbed me and threw me to the ground. They tied my hands to the back of the jeep. One of them got into the jeep and started to drive it, like they were going to drag me, like you see in the old cowboy movies. They only drove the jeep two or three feet. I knew they were not going to drag me.

We were handcuffed and they drove us to the MP station. They put us in a barbed wired fence-in area. They called my company and told them where we were. The Lieutenant came down and told us our company moved out an hour ago and the captain is really pissed off at us. We went back to base camp; got our equipment and they flew us out to where our company was.

We saw our Sergeant and he told us, "The captain is really mad at you two. He wants you two to be point men, from now, until we go back into base camp. I don't like it; I think he is trying to get you guys killed. But I am not losing my stripes over you guys screwing up. You got caught and this is the problem."

We pulled point for about 5 days, just Vontor and I, together. We took turns, when he was tired, I would take over, when I was tired, he would take over, all day long. A point man chops the foliage to make a path through the jungle. A soldier is behind me, with a compass, telling me which direction to go.

When we went back to base camp the captain wanted to see us. We went up to his tent. He said he was really upset with us. He was going to give us an article 15, if you don't want that, we will give you a court-martial. Vontor was upset, he said, "I'll take the court-martial. My mother just died of cancer, right before I was drafted, and everyone around here is getting killed."

I signed the Article 15 right away. I said to Timmy, "You have to sign the Article 15, a court-martial will follow you the rest of your life, you'll never get a job." He signed the Article 15. I think about that now and think he should have taken the court martial, because less than a month later, he was killed, fighting on top of a tank, while shooting a machine gun, an M60, on July 9, 1966.

Two days later, we went out into the jungle for 8 or 9 days, nothing really happed out there, so they flew us back in helicopters. They picked us up with trucks called deuce and a half. We got on the truck and I was one of the last one to get a seat on the truck. Going back to our tents, we drove by the MPs mess hall. Somebody said that is the MPs mess hall, let's throw some grenades at them. Somebody said, "No, let's just throw smoke grenades and tear gas grenades. You don't want to kill any of those assholes." They threw about ten. Someone asked me for my gas grenade and they threw it out towards the mess hall.

We went back to our tents and fifteen minutes later, they told us to come up to the road and leave your weapons back in the tent. We all lined up in standing formation. About twenty MPs were standing there with gas-masks on, and the ones who didn't have gas masks, their eyes were watering. The captain started yelling at us. The captain sounded like a real ass. He was upset and said to us, "You should be ashamed of yourselves. That is your parents' tax money going to waste." He wanted to know who threw the tear gas grenades. Nobody said anything. One of the MPs said something to Captain Lupus. Then the captain called out my name, Vontor and a bible-reading mild guy from Kentucky. I found out later, he was very upset when he lost some friends in his squad. He went into town and started drinking. When MPs pulled up, he started fighting with them.

I told him, "I didn't do it. Somebody asked for my tear gas grenade and I gave it to him." Who did you give it to? I said, "I don't know." Then someone volunteered and said they did it. I don't know what happened to him. Over the phone, I talked to a friend, Saunders, from Kentucky, and he thought the

Lieutenants volunteered, and said they threw the grenades at the MP's mess hall; but I don't remember that.

Leg Cramps

About July 7th or 8th, 1966 at night, we were out on an operation for about a week, on ambush patrol, on a search and destroy mission. It was hot and dry and I got cramps in my legs and my back. I fell out and a medic, by the name of Vernie (Doc-Foggy) Williams came over to me and told the Lieutenant he was sending me back to base camp. The lieutenant told Captain Lukas, and the captain said, "No, we don't want him to leave, we need everyone." The Doc said, "No, he is going back. I have the last say out here in the field, who stays and who goes, I am the medic." So, they sent me back on the next helicopter that was resupplying us. I saw Vontor before I left and I said I was leaving because my legs cramped up. He said, "Let me have your fatigues. My fatigues had my name on it, Cubbage, and on top of my name in small print it had, Cubit, (that's how the Vietnamese spell and pronounce my name.) I said, "My fatigues are dirty," Vontor said, "My fatigues are dirtier than yours." I said, "Okay," and we exchanged fatigues.

The helicopters came down and resupplied our company, and I left with them. The next morning, I got up and I went to sick call. I told the doctor what happened about cramping up and he asked, "How much water do you drink"? I said, "I don't know," "How many canteens do you have"? I said, "I have two." He said, "Well get another canteen." He asked me, "Do you take salt tablets"? I said, "Yes, when they give them to me." "Well, here is a box of salt tablets. Do you take iodine tablets"? I said, "Sometimes, when they give them to me." "Well, here is a box of iodine tablets. Put two in your canteen when you get water from the stream." (As if I didn't know that)

Battle of Minh Thanh Road, July 9, 1966

After seeing the doctor, I went back to my tent and a guy from the CP came running into the tent and said, "Cubbage, your name came over the radio saying that you were killed. I told them I saw you in your tent earlier. Is someone wearing your fatigues"? I said, "Oh shit, Vontor."

He turned around and ran back up to the CP. I ran up to the Command Post too. I could hear gunfire, fighting and people yelling on their radio.

I was upset and very emotional and turned around and went back to my tent.

A couple of days later my Company came back in, from being out in the field, a lot of soldiers were killed: Pfc Thomas Vontor, Pfc James Brown and Sp4 Gyorgy Besze were in my squad. Four tanks were hit by mortars and got knocked out. Vontor was sitting on top of one of them. They said he was shooting the machine gun when he got hit by mortars. Sgt. Charles De Jean III was also killed in that battle.

The sergeant came in and said, "Cubbage, Captain Lupus wants to see you up in the CP." I went up to the CP and went in to see the captain. I did not salute him. He said, "What was Vontor doing with your fatigues on"? I said. "He wanted them, his were dirty and he wanted mine." The captain said, "Yours are dirty too." I told him that, and Vontor said, "Well yours are not as dirty as mine," so I gave them to him. The captain then said, "I could have notified your family that you were killed, you know that, don't you?" He said, "Get out of here, go back to your tent." I went back to my tent, an hour later, someone from the CP said the captain wants everyone to put their name inside their boots. The captain said, "You may give your fatigues away, but you are not going to give your boots away."

The next day the sergeant said, "I asked the captain if you could take Vontor home." The captain said, "I don't think Cubbage would come back." The sergeant said, "If Cubbage says he will come back, he will come back." Then the captain told the sergeant, "I can't afford to have anyone leave now, I am under 80 men."

I was really upset with the captain because I could have escorted my friend, Tommy Vontor, home. He liked to be called Timmy, instead of Tommy, I don't know why.

About a week later the whole company was out on patrol and the captain walked by and saw me and he stopped to say, "Cubbage, I am going to take that Article 15 away from you and Vontor." I yelled at him, "I don't give a f**k about that article 15. I just want to get the f**k out of here. I am tired of everyone being killed." Young and Greer said, "You really got the captain mad by yelling at him, we were waiting for you to shoot him."

I was depressed that another one of my friends got killed. Too many of my friends were being slaughtered and blown apart on the battlefield. Fear and anxiety were building up in me to a point I could no longer tolerate it. I had no patience left for a captain who wanted to take away our article 15, after my buddy died, who cares.

Afterwards, I felt the captain wanted to make friends with me, but I was too upset, I didn't want to be bothered with him. My friends said he wanted to make friends but you messed it up by yelling at him.

At the end of the month I got a pay voucher that said, "**NPD**" on it, which meant, "**No Pay Due**" because of my article 15. I spent two months in a combat zone, and I did not get paid for it.

A few days later we were on a road clearance and they said a tank blew up down the road and they wanted us to secure the tank until they can get somebody to repair it. We walked down the road and treads on the tank had been blown off. There wasn't anybody around. This was the first time I saw my captain since, I swore at him, and told him what I thought of him, and his article 15. He walked up and looked at the tank.

I said, "Yo, cap, Mom wasn't too mad at the tear gas grenades that were thrown at the MP's mess hall, but wait until she gets this f**king bill, she will be really pissed off." The captain was really mad at me now, he just walked away from me.

The Wire

The lieutenant said to me, "Cubbage, you and these three guys follow this wire, that blew up the tank, down to see where it leads to." It led down and across an open football-size field into the jungle. Livingston from South Carolina, Carlson from Ohio, and a new guy who I don't remember came with me. I thought to myself, "Why was I picked to go the f**k down there, instead of the lieutenant or sergeant, and just four of us?"

We followed the wire down to the jungle. Then we entered into the jungle, following the wire across the creek. I looked back at the tank and I couldn't see the tank from where we were. I knew they couldn't see us, and we couldn't see them. I said to the guys, "STOP, we are not going any further. There could be a 100 VC up there where the wire leads to, or there could be 10 VC waiting to ambush us. We are going to cut the wire here, and tell the lieutenant that we couldn't find anything."

All at once, we could hear the sound of artillery coming in towards us. We turned around and started running through the creek. Two or three explosions from the artillery hit the ground. A piece of shrapnel hit Carlson in the leg. His leg swelled up and was bleeding. I ran out and started waving my hands and yelling, "We're back here, STOP, STOP THAT!" They only dropped two or three artillery rounds, then they stopped. I ran back to get Carlson. Livingston and I carried him out into the open. Livingston put a tourniquet around Carlson's leg. I started yelling for a medic. Everyone ran down to us, it looked like the whole company came running down. The medic was fixing Carlson up and he started yelling at Captain Lemus, "I hope you die, and I hope your mother dies of f**king cancer, I hope you get f**king killed." I started yelling at the captain too, "You tried to get us f**king killed. You knew we were in there." He said, "I didn't try to get anyone killed, I thought you went to the left." "Bullshit, you sent us down there. You knew we were there, you piece of shit." Carlson was still screaming at him as they evacuated him to a hospital. I never knew what happened to Carlson after that, he never came back.

A week or two later Captain Lukas left and was replaced by Captain Downs. He stayed with us until he got wounded on August 25th. Guess who they brought back….

The sergeant said to me, "You missed a big fight when Vontor got killed, we had four guys that got killed, and five guys got wounded. We only have a seven-man squad. Guys were always being replaced. You and I are doing good, so far, in our squad. Adam drown, Bechtel was killed, along with Vontor, James Brown, and Hollifield."

Highway 13, Thunder Road, Ambush Alley

We took part in numerous missions to safeguard American supply convoys moving on Highway 13. A typical operation includes a daily sweep through tiny villages that dot the route, gouging out the sides of the road to cut hidden wires and clearing road blocks often booby trapped or mined.

Highway 13, nicknamed "Thunder Road" and "Ambush Alley" snakes north of Saigon through sunbaked paddy fields, dark rubber plantations and dense jungle undergrowth.

The 'thunder' of the road is the roar of Communist mines as they blast into our passing military vehicles. The hidden explosives, often detonated by wires leading hundreds of yards away from the highway.

They are a chilling fact of life for American supply columns that travel Route 13 to the U.S. Army brigades at Lai Khe and Phuoc Vinh.

The battle of Minh Thanh Road was one of the most violent and deadly actions of the war, so far, that took place on July 9, 1966, near the Minh Thanh rubber plantation. On that day a task force comprised of Company B and Company C and 4th Calvary were attacked by the Viet Cong, 272nd Regiment. The fight lasted three hours. They said it was bitter and short. It began shortly before noon and was over three hours later as the Viet Cong broke contact.

Medic Vernie Williams

These are the exact words of Medic Vernie (Doc-Foggy) Williams from Compton, California describing the events of July 9, 1966.

The day before this battle this medic saved my life by sending me back to Base Camp in Phuoc Vin. I would have been beside my good friend Vontor, and other friends who were killed in company 'B', this day.

"Conversion…. From Combat Medic to Combat Infantryman"

Many years ago, while undergoing my Army Basic Training, I decided I'd never make a good Infantryman. Fortunately, they chose to train me as a Medic. Six years later found me in Vietnam, not just a Medic, but in a rifle company with the 1st Battalion 2nd Infantry of the 1st Infantry Division. Six months of Air Assaults, Night Ambushes, Search and Destroy Missions, saw me unscratched, and never having fired my Army issued .45 automatic pistol. Fear of death had become a non-issue, having learned to live from moment to moment, day-to-day, doing my job almost without thinking. I'd adjusted to living in that Mad…Mad…World!

Early July, 1966, the battalion was about to end a somewhat non-productive Search and Destroy Mission, and head back "home" to out base camp, when we were told that 100 men were needed to support the ¾ Armored Cavalry Squadron of our division. Boy was I pissed! It meant me putting off my planned R&R trip to the Philippines. The only consolation was that we'd at least be riding atop tanks or armored personnel carriers. Great relief to our backs and feet. Sure enough, by that afternoon we'd met up with the Cav, climbed aboard and headed to their main assembly point, outside a small Vietnamese village. That spot was where we ate, slept, played cards, and drank warm beer for two whole days. A mini R&R. Then one evening, a Commanders call took place, and our mission explained. The next morning, July 9th, we would convoy down Route 13 (aka Thunder Road). The two Troops would be separated about one (1) kilometer apart. G-2 (Intelligence) expected us to be hit by a battalion sized unit, so we were ordered to load up twice the amount of ammo, and Medics also to carry extra supplies. I was scheduled to be in that lead Troop.

Next morning all the tanks and armored personnel carriers cranked up and roared into position on the road, almost making me feel like I was back in Fulda, Germany with the 14th Armored Cavalry. The order was given and we moved out on that dirt road called a highway. Miles went by without one shot fired at us by even one lone sniper. Some stretches of the road had clear visibility on both sides, while others had thick, heavy growth, wall-high to the very edge of the road. There we couldn't see over, around, or through it. Through one such patch, suddenly over the radio, the point vehicle called out saying he was taking heavy small arms automatic fire. The Commander ordered the column to speed up and race to his aide. That move sprung the trap. Suddenly we were being fired upon from all sides… completely surrounded! Sound of bullets clanging against the vehicles sides, then explosions of incoming mortars and R.P.G.'s. The noise was deafening. Both sides were almost firing point-blank at each other without visual contact! Armor's strategy was to keep moving, minimizing chances of a stationery, large target. So, the drivers would pull forward, stop suddenly, spin around, and back up. Soon the cries for Medic sounded out from a nearby vehicle. Our driver sped to it, and I jumped over on it to start my work. Several soldiers were wounded, but none had life or limb threatening conditions. I was finished within minutes. However, by that time, both vehicles were widely separated and the only way I could get back to mine was to run for it. I decided to stay where I was. I chose to pick up one wounded soldier's M-14 and start firing, my first time firing and M-14. The young soldier acted as my loader, and I the gunner sweeping the thick, surrounding brush with automatic fire in bursts of 3 to 5. We went through boxes of ammo in no time, and by then the barrel was hot and smoking.

During one re-loading pause, I was accidentally slammed against the barrel when our driver made one of his quick, unexpected moves. A burn resulted. When we completely ran out of ammo, I climbed atop the vehicle and started forward. Suddenly I was hit with something that knocked me back down inside and my whole left arm went numb. No real pain, only total numbness. Trying to gather myself, I noticed my loader yelling something and pointing at that left arm. Glancing over I discovered my sleeve had been torn away, and I had a gash in that arm larger than my fist. That white "thing" I saw was bone! Skin, muscle, and tissue was gone. Later I realized that 2 inches more to the left or to the right might have been a complete miss OR the arm being blown off! Calmly I said to my loader…" You're the Medic now, and I need help!" I opened the first battle dressing and instructed him how exactly how to apply and tie it. Just as he was about to apply the second one, a flash and explosion hit us. I don't remember if I totally blacked out or not, but his time I felt pain, my ears ringing, and discovering blood mainly from my right shoulder down that arm. That right eardrum was perforated and I had been peppered with shrapnel from my head downward. We guessed it to be and RPG or Recoilless rifle shell that had penetrated the walls and exploded inside. The Track Commander had been blown out of his hatch and killed or captured. All of us hit with the shrapnel except the driver. Our radio was knocked out, but neither the engine nor the track was damaged. Before our driver could get us away, we took one more glancing hit, which failed to penetrate or do damage. Our driver then managed to get us to the rear where he was directed to keep going to where the trailing troops Medic was using his vehicle as an aid-station. Minutes later we did reach that aid-station, where our driver dropped us off, and the Senior Medic did his work applying dressings and giving Morphine where needed. Even under morphine y adrenalin was still flowing, and I couldn't sit or lie down while sounds of battle continued all around me. But before I could leave the aid-station, a vehicle came roaring in, its lights on, horn blowing, and soldiers frantically waving their arms. The driver slammed to a stop, backed as close as he could, then dropped the ramp. Two soldiers drug a shirtless comrade by his arms and dropped him at my feet. I could see that one eye was missing, while the other was wide open with a fixed dazed toward the sky. He looked to be in shock. From the bottom of his rib-cage to below his navel was one gigantic hole. Intestines were dragging in the red Vietnamese dirt. Reaching over I grasped his trembling hand and felt his last earthly move. A feeble squeezed of my hand, before relaxing in death. I lay that lifeless hand on his chest. His buddy looked at my face, begging reassurance. All I could do was signal… "Thumbs Down"! When his sobbing stopped, the soldier approached me and explained what had happened. Apparently, a VC soldier unexpectedly jumped from his hidden foxhole, sprinted to their Vehicle and tossed in a grenade, before being cut down by a GI's M-16. Somebody yelled, "Grenade," but too late to pick it up and throw it out, so one young soldier did the only think he could do. Fall on it and smother the blast with his own body. Quick and easy.

Despite that tragedy, I still needed to stay alive, so I first picked up an M-79 Grenade Launcher and went back to work. No, I'd never fired one before. But it was just like loading and firing a shotgun. Break it open, drop in a shell, re-join the two sections and fire. I did so until running short of shells. Then somebody handed me an M-16, which I used until the word came to "Cease Fire"! How long that battle lasted I don't know. But it felt like all day. Apparently, the VC had enough, so they pulled out. That evening I was on a chopper being flown to an Army MASH hospital where I had my first of what would be five surgeries. Several days later while reading about the battle in Stars & Stripes I realized it was my 28th birthday. The newspaper said that we had battled a VC regiment, and that the lead troop was "Bait." My best buddy Emette Duggans from Virginia was among those killed that day. Thanks to an M-14, M-16, M-79, M-113 Armored Personnel Carrier, and its courageous young driver, I survived. I have great respect for Infantrymen, but I'm still glad that I was and Army Medic.

The Mamasan

After July 9th, Aaron Whitaker came over and said, "Let's go into town and we'll have fun, drinking and partying a little bit with the girls. They had cat houses in Phuoc Vinh. I'll take care of everything. He came over that night and he had a sack of frozen chicken and sea rations to give to the girls. He said we'll sneak into town. It was dark. We went to a cat house. When we went inside, two soldiers were in there, one had his shirt off, he reminded me of my friend, Bruno, from Philly. He was a muscular guy who lifted weights or he was in artillery. I thought to myself, he is going to be a problem. He was drunk and rugged looking. One of the guys went into one of the rooms. We saw the mamasan, then Whitaker put his rifle down and started talking to her. He left the sack of food there, and said we'll come back. He was picking up his own rifle and the muscular guy said, "If you touch that rifle, I'll shoot you." Whitaker said, "That's my rifle, I am responsible for it." The guy said, "I don't care, leave it there." Then I walked behind the guy and stuck my M16 rifle in his back. I said, "I don't want to shoot you, but I will, if you shoot him, I'll f...ing shoot you. Don't even try to turn around."

The mamasan grabbed his rifle and said, "Come with me, we go boom, boom." He went into the back room with her. Whitaker grabbed his rifle and said "Let's go."

I walked outside backwards, with my rifle in my hand because I didn't trust him. We got outside and we both agreed he looked like trouble. He wasn't from our company; he was probably from artillery. Then we sneaked back to our base camp. Things like that happened.

I Had a Good Dog

We came back to Phuoc Vin and we took a shower with 500 gallon- barrels of water. We took cold showers. We just got done and it was one of the few times that we found out we were going to get passes to go into Phuoc Vinh. The captain was going to let us go for the day. We had to be back by 7:00 pm.

A cook came over to me and said let's go into town and see some mamasans and have some beer. We went down to the village and started going into a couple of bars. We saw a bar that was called, Elvis Presley Bar, we laughed about the name. We went inside and asked them if they had any food to eat. They said, yes, and they gave us something that looked like a menu. It had ribs and rice and other stuff. Whitaker ordered ribs and rice and I said give me the same thing. We ordered another beer, 33 Beer, pronounced "Ba Muoi Ba" which means thirty-three in Vietnamese. They brought out the ribs and rice. We started eating them and they were small. Whitaker said, "Aren't ribs from pigs, shouldn't they be bigger than this?" I joked, "The people here are little, so maybe the pigs are little too." We ate them and had another beer.

We decided to leave and go back to camp. Whitaker wanted to go back another way. They had a black section of town and a white section of town. When you were out in the jungle everyone got along, but in camp sometimes, we had racial problems. Any time a black and white person fought they called it racial.

Two whites could fight it wasn't racial, two blacks could fight, it wasn't racial.

We walked through the black part of town and went down this one street, we passed by a bar that had a sign on it. Whitaker said, "Look at that." He went over and grabbed the sign and showed it to me. It said no whites allowed. I said, "Who cares?" He said, "Well, that's not right. We don't have signs saying no n*****s allowed in our part of town." I said, "You don't like it?" He said, "No," I said, "We'll do something about it." I took the sign from him and I walked over to the door where there was a gook outside taking everybody's weapon away from them and giving them a number to get their rifle back. I pushed him aside and walked into the bar with Whitaker behind me. Music was playing, everyone was dancing and rocking and rolling. Everything stopped when we walked in. I put my rifle on the bar and placed the sign on top. I said, "Give us two beers." Everything was quiet then, I looked around and I saw some black friends from my company and some I did not know. My friend, Sgt. Richard Glenn "the Bird" from Philadelphia, came over to me and said, "I'll buy you a beer." I said, "No, I'll buy it." He said, "Cub, you can't buy a beer in here. You know what I mean?" And I did, I knew they didn't want me to buy a beer in their bar. We had a beer and we talked. I took out my money and I said, "I'll buy the next round." He said "No, Cub, I'm paying for this round and the next one too. You're not buying a drink in here." I said, "Okay." I had a second drink then we left. A few of the black GIs in the bar were mad because a white person came in with a rifle, and they didn't like it. No whites went into that bar to buy a drink, before me.

We left and walked back to Phuoc Vinh. I went back to my tent and Whitaker went back to his tent. About an hour later somebody came into my tent and said, "Cubbage, are you friends with that cook from Philadelphia? They took him out and evacuated him to a medevac. They think he has appendicitis."

I got up and went about a mile down to his tent. I walked in and I saw a Sgt who was a cook there, I asked, "Is Whitaker here?" He said, "No, they took him to the hospital, they think he has appendicitis." Are you from Philly? I said, "Yes." "Are you two stealing chickens from us"? I said, "I don't know what you're talking about"? He said, "Well, I heard Whitaker and a friend from Philly were the ones who stole the chickens. We are going to catch him stealing those chickens and he is going to be out in the field like you are, and he is going to get his ass killed." I said, "Sgt, I don't know what you are talking about, I'll see you." I left.

About a week later, Whitaker told me, "I didn't have appendicitis, they pumped my stomach and they found out I had food poisoning. They said I ate a bad dog." I laughed and said, "My dog must have been a good dog because I didn't get sick." I told Whitaker what his Sgt said, and that he wanted to put him out in the field with me. Whitaker said, "He doesn't know it's me, he can't prove it, he just thinks it's me."

Johnny Moore, My Native American Friend

Our company was out on patrol and our quad was leading the company, we were beating the bush. I heard gunfire and I thought I heard someone yell sniper. I hit the ground and I heard someone yell, "It's a snake!" I thought it was a small snake, like a rattler. I got up and walked over to it. It was a gigantic python; he was digesting something big in his stomach. We looked at it, it was just lying there. Johnny Moore said, "I can make a belt out of that snake. Anybody want to carry it for me back to base camp? I'll skin it and dry it out. And I'll make belts for everyone." Some guys took a machete and cut down a big limb off a tree. They wrapped the snake around the limb. The limb of the tree was thick and about 7 foot long. They started carrying it through the jungles for about 20 minutes. Johnny Moore was on point. The two guys got tired and they decided not to carry it any more. Vontor and I started carrying it for another 20 or 30 minutes. It was really heavy; the snake must have weighed more than a hundred pounds. We said we are not going to carry it either. It was hard carrying it through the jungle. We put it down and we kept on going through the jungle for another hour before we came to our camp site where we were camping for the night. We used to say to Johnny, "Where is my belt"? He said, "It is out in the jungle where you left it."

One time, on patrol, from the jungles we went into a village with our platoon. The lieutenant, Sgt. Jackson, TK Stone, Vontor, Johnny Moore, (a Native American from Oklahoma). The village was pretty big. It had over a hundred hooches. We gathered people up so we could count them. Johnny Moore, Vontor and I went down this small road when a gook came out of a hooch, and said to us. "Me no VC, me no VC, me no VC, me cowboy." We stopped him and we had our rifles pointed at him and he said again, "Me no VC, me no VC, you want to boomboom?" Johnny Moore said to us, he was just a pimp. He said, "No, I am just a cowboy. You want to boomboom my sister"? With that, Johnny punched him in his face. The gook backs up, starts to run away, then falls into a well. We yelled down into the well but we didn't hear anything, so we just left. The lieutenant asked us did anything happen, we said no, nothing happened. Later we got on the helicopter and left. We often talked about it and wondered, did he jump into the well, or did he fall into the well because he didn't see it?

A few weeks later, Johnny Moore's father died when we were out in the field. Another soldier by the same name of Johnny Moore, and also from Oklahoma, not related to each other, was back in base camp. When Johnny Moore's father died the other Johnny Moore took the emergency leave papers and flew home to Oklahoma for seven days. He said he didn't look at the papers until he got home, and realized it was not his father who had died. When he went back to Vietnam, Johnny Moore was furious at him.

Captain Lupus said, "It is one of those things, we can't let him go home now, because the emergency papers were already used and his father was already buried." They transferred my friend, Johnny Moore, to another company because there was a rumor that he was going to shoot the captain and the other Johnny Moore, the next time they were out in combat together. I hope Johnny is doing well in Oklahoma.

That was the same captain who would not let me go home to accompany my friend, Vontor, when he was killed.

The Weather, Red Ants, and Wait-A-Minute Bushes

I am sitting here thinking about Vietnam. I spent 365 days in Vietnam and at least 320 days, I spent in the boonies or the jungles. Every night we had to dig foxholes, sometimes we would dig them 4 feet deep. Whenever we made no contact with the enemy, we would only dig two feet deep. The next morning, we would have to fill the hole back up again, before we could leave. Also, every night we put out claymore mines, which would blow fire steel balls out to about 110 yards within a 60-degree arc in front of the device. It is used primarily in ambushes and as an anti-infiltration device against enemy infantry. We would always laugh, because it had printed on the front, "This Side Toward Enemy." We also put flares out with string wrapped around them. If the VC tripped the string, the flare would go up, and we could see them. That happened about four times during the year.

We went weeks and sometimes months without any resistance or combat. Then all at once everything would happen and all hell broke loose. Every time the enemy would attack us, a few of our soldiers got wounded or killed.

There are two types of seasons in Vietnam, 105/110 degrees hot and dry and the hot and wet, which is the monsoon season. During the monsoon season it would rain every day, and every night it would pour. You would put your poncho over your fox hole to stay dry but you still got soaked. When the sun went down it would drop from 110 degrees to 80 degrees, you were wet and cold. A big drop of 30 degrees made you shiver all night long. You didn't realize you could feel the cold so much when it was only 80 degrees and soaking wet.

I also remember the red ants. They would fall down from the trees and crawl onto your neck and bite you, and crawl up your legs and bite you hard, really hurt. When you were under fire the red ants would fall on you and bite you, anyone who was there knows what I am talking about. I am sure some guys got shot by jumping up, to get away from the red ants.

When you are going through the jungles, some guys would get stuck on a heavy, thorny bush, and they would say, "Hey, wait-a-minute, I am stuck on this bush.

One time, we were going through the jungles, we started receiving enemy fire. We walked into an ambush. I fell down and a new guy, who just came into our platoon and I didn't know him at the time, got stuck on the wait-a-minute-bushes. I got up and grabbed him and threw him down on the ground. He always told everybody that I saved his life that day. His name is Thomas Young. After that, we became good friends for the rest of our time in Vietnam. He is either from New York or South Carolina, he lived in both places.

I met a soldier in Vietnam when he came out into the field. His name was Pfc Reynolds. I asked him if he is related to the Reynolds Aluminum foil. He said, "I don't think so, I could be. My father owns 50,000 acres of cattle land in Montana.

I have been flying a helicopter since I was 12 years old." I said, "Get out of here." He said, "We all fly when we are young." His father and brother taught him how to fly and he got his license to fly when he was 16, before he got his driver's license. He and his father were writing letters to their congressmen and generals to let him fly helicopters. One day the captain told him he was going to flight school. He said, "I'll see you, and he gave me a hug goodbye." I never went to Montana but I would like to see him again, He should be easy to find, a Reynolds with a 50,000-acre cattle farm.

Low-Grade Gunpowder

When in fire-fights, a lot of times, our M16s or the AR15s would jam when you put it on automatic. They said it could fire twenty rounds of ammunition in $5/10^{th}$ of a second, which meant it would fire before you could say 'automatic'. The rifles started to jam because they substituted low-grade gun powder to save money. The Congressmen made millions of dollars by buying stock in war materials and substituting low grade gun powder. Fifty-eight thousand soldiers died because of their greed.

.50 Caliber Machine Gun

In March, 1966, the captain thought we would have more fire power if he issued us a .50 caliber machine gun. It weighed about 84 pounds and the tripod weighed 44 pounds. When we carried it through the jungle, we had to disassemble it into four pieces, each man carried one part. The tripod was the heaviest. We carried it for two weeks when we got into a fire fight. Before we could use it, we had to put the .50 caliber machine gun back together. None of the four guys who were carrying the four pieces of the .50 caliber machine gun were near each other when we got into the fire fight. It would have taken twenty minutes to put the .50 caliber machine gun back together, and by then the fire fight would be over. Therefore, we could never use it, it was not practical.

Captain Lupus decided they would bring the machine gun down to us by helicopter when they resupplied us at nighttime. We weren't resupplied every night, sometimes they would come once a week. Then they just stopped bringing the .50 caliber machine gun down to us.

The same captain gave us an infrared telescope. When we went out on ambush patrol at nighttime it was really nice to have. With a little bit of moon light, I could see the animals moving at nighttime. I liked it. I would have happily carried it. But the captain took it from us because he said if the enemy got their hands on it, they would have an advantage over us. I went down to the supply sergeant and asked if I could have one and he said there were only two issued to our company and the captain told him not to let anyone have one. This was another reason I never got along with this captain.

I Met Friends from Swampoodle in Vietnam

When we were out on a search and patrol mission, if we find any tunnels, we would check to see if there was any information inside the tunnel. Then we would destroy the tunnel. They told us to take a break because the 9th Light Infantry Division was coming through and they said "just relax." I sat down on my helmet and lit a cigarette. Then I heard, "Hey Cubbage, how are you doing?" I looked up and there was a guy from my neighborhood, by the name of Bob "Monk" Feeney, he was passing through. I knew his brother Jackie Feeney better than Monk. I stood up, shook hands, and we talked about our neighborhood for a couple of minutes, shook hands again, and we wished each other luck, and we'll see each other back in Philly.

After I came out of Vietnam, got married, and moved to Mayfair, I met him again at Mayfair Athletic Club, MAC. We became friends and I helped him coach baseball little league. He was a

Philadelphia policeman. He died of agent orange, twenty years after he left Vietnam.

A few weeks later we were in the jungle and the fourth infantry walked through. I met another guy I knew from Swampoodle, named Rub Herron. I told him a few weeks ago I met Monk Feeney. He said he knew him. We said what do you think the odds are that we would meet someone from our neighborhood, **Swampoodle**, passing by in the jungles of Vietnam, **8,693 miles away**. He said there are a lot of guys here from **Swampoodle**. After the service, Rub got a hold of me, and we had him for dinner, at our house in Mayfair. He had some problems, divorced his pretty wife, Peggy Crow, and he later died. I think he died from agent orange, less than ten years after being in Vietnam.

Guys from Swampoodle who Served in Vietnam

1. Edmond J. Cubbage, 1965-67, Army, Airborne, Big Red One
2. James Fogarty, 1965-67, Army 173rd, Airborne Brigade
3. Patrick Cubbage, 1969, 173rd Airborne Brigade
4. Dennis Egan, 1966-67, US Marines 3rdBattalion7th

5. Michael Egan, 1969-70, 1st/82nd field artillery
6. Frank LaBletta, 1966-68, Army, 1st Calvary Division, Airmobile
7. Frank Gallagher, 1965-67, 4th Infantry
8. Bobbie Brooke, 1965-67, Army
9. Bobby McCullough, 1965-67, 101st
10. Alfred Lauer, 1965-1967 Army, 9th Division 39th Infantry
11. Frank Fullam, 1960-1966 Marines MP
12. Charles LaFontano, 1964, 499th ARS
13. Charles (Chuck) Quinn, 1968-70, USS MarsAFS-1
14. Tom Holland, 1970-71, 24th Evac Hospital Long Binh
15. Larry Greene Sr, 1969-70, 35th Engineers
16. John Shields, MACV, 1965-67 Advisory Team 96
17. Michael Walsh, Army, 1965-67, RIP
18. Mark Opsliski, 1967-68, 7th Cav, Artillery
19. Joey Geary, Army, Vietnam, (David Croce's cousin).
20. John Cappello, Army, 1968-70
21. Edward (Bud) Donahue, Army, 1965-66
22. Tommy Powers, 1965-67, 173rd
23. Carl "Skippy" Wallace, 1968-70, 173rd
24. James Rodden, Air Force, 1967-68

25. Robert L DeCarlo, Army, 1966-67
26. Frank Rowland, Army, 1965-66
27. Bob Brady, Army, 1967
28. Walter Mahoney, US Navy, Ret, 1967-1998
29. Walter J. Miller, Army, 1966-71 Died of Agent Orange
30. Edward Slavin, Jr., 1966-68 Army, 25th Infantry, Agt. Orange
31. Alex DiGiacomo, 1966-67, Sgt. USMC
32. Alfred Lauer, 1966-67 Army, 9th Division, 39th Infantry
33. Benjamin Stacey, 1965-67, Airforce
34. Billy Garvin, 1965-67, Airforce
35. Pat "Doc" Dougherty, 1968-70, Army
36. John Cubbage, 1965-69, Navy
37. Jay Sanders, 1965-69, Navy
38. Albert Torcini, 1965-67, Marines
39. Larry Greene, 1969-70, Army
40. Pat Grugan, 1965-67, Army, 173rd Airborne, Medic
41. Richard Simpson, 1965-67, Army
42. John Everly, 1965-67, Airborne Ranger
43. Joe Van Heusen, 1965-67, Army, Ranger
44. Jim Columbo, 1967-68, USMC
45. Bob (Monk) Feeney, 1965-67, Army
46. Robert (Rub) Hearne, 1965-67, Army
47. Jack Kite, 1969-70, Army, MP

48. Jimmy Burns, 1968-70, Army, Dog Trainer
49. Harry Hessian, 1965-67, Marines
50. Billy Joyce, 1965-67, Marine
51. Bing Brown, 1967-68
52. Chuck Curcio, 1965-67, Marine
53. James Rodgers, 1967-68, Army

KIA

54. Vince Garvey, 1966, Army Airborne, KIA on Oct. 7, 1966.
55. Patrick Thiroway, Military Police, KIA on May 19, 1968
56. Matthew Higgins, Army 4th Infantry, KIA on March 14, 1967
57. Joseph Edward Sweeney, Army, 173rd Airborne, KIA on May 29, 1971. (Jimmy Sweeney-McWhorter's cousin)
58. Victor Spadaro, 1966, Marines

Swampoodle Veterans Who Served but Did Not Go to Vietnam

- Jim McWhorter, Army, 1965-67, Turkey
- Bruno Rosica, 1966-1968, Army, Oklahoma
- Kevin McGinn, 1967-69, Army, Boxing Team in Massachusetts

- John (Ozzie) Auerswald, 1965-68, Navy, California
- Joseph Mossop, 1969-71, Army, Oklahoma
- Chuck Mahoney, 1965, Army Reserves
- George Hanlon, 1965-67, Marine Reserves
- Tommy Higgins, 1965-67, Army
- Ed Collins, 1964-66, Army, Germany
- Ronnie Cubbage, 1963-66, Marines, Japan
- John Stem, 1963-65, Air Force
- Billy Kelly, 1965-85, Army
- Frank Martin, WW II, 1944-1945, Army Air Corps & Friend

Sgt. Tahike, Sgt. Jackson, Sgt. DeJean, Sgt. Rivera

Spec 4 Tahika became our sergeant after Sgt Jackson got killed. Two weeks later he was rotated out of Vietnam because his year was up. He and TK Stone left at the same time.

Sgt. Charles DeJean III became our Sgt. He was stationed at the Vietnam Headquarters for a while before coming to our company. He wasn't a bad guy. When we went out, he listened to the guys, and tried to avoid contact with the enemy. He was killed during the July 9th battle, along with my friend, Vontor, and other friends.

Then we got Sgt. Rivera, he just arrived in the country. He was not related to my other friend, Lou Rivera. There were about 3 or 4 Riveras in my company. That's a common name. I tried tracking down my friend, Lou, in New York but there were too many Riveras in the phone book.

TK Stone

I want to tell you a story about TK Stone. We came back from the field and I went into my tent. A guy, James Brown, said to me, I think TK took your jump boots and went home with them. I looked in my locker, which was made out of beer cans, and my jump boots were gone. There was an envelope in there and it said, "Cub, I took your boots and I am going back to Seattle. I know you'll be mad at me for stealing your jump boots, but I know you will be happy knowing, I was going home. When you leave just steal someone else's boots. TK." I went up to Brown and I asked him, "Why did you let him steal my boots?" I told him, "If Cubbage catches you, stealing them, he is going to shoot you." He answered, "If Cubbage wants them back, I'll give them back to him in Seattle." Brown said, "TK Stone left yesterday," while we were out in the field.

Another incident; we were going by a rice paddy about a football field away, and there was a farmer out there, with his water buffalo. The first sergeant said, "Hey, look at them over there, do you think anyone could shoot that water buffalo from here?" TK Stone immediately aimed his M14 rifle at the water buffalo and shot it. We all watched and saw the buffalo just drop over into the rice paddies. The first sergeant yelled, "Hey, I didn't want anyone to shoot it, I was just wondering." We all laughed and said, "You don't have to wonder anymore."

About a week later Captain Downs came down and said, "No more shooting any water buffaloes. We have to pay the farmer for the buffalo you shot. We do not have a good relationship with the farmers and everyone around here. We have to improve our relationship with the farmers." We found out later that the First Sergeant took responsibility for killing the buffalo, that's why TK Stone did not get an article 15.

About 25 years later when I was in Seattle with my daughter, Donna, I tried to look up TK Stone in the phone book. I couldn't find him. My Donna noticed they had a Vietnam Traveling Wall at a park close to where we were staying. We went over to the wall and I started looking for visitors who had hats or shirts with the Big Red One printed on it. I met a guy that had a Big Red One on his hat and I asked him, "Is your name TK Stone"? He said, "No." We started talking for a while about Vietnam. He said to me, "I know a guy by the name of Travis Stone at the VA hospital." I then gave him my name and phone number and asked him to give it to TK Stone. I also said, "He stole my boots 25 years ago. Let him know I am not mad at him, and give me a phone call."

About two months later in Philly I got a phone call from TK Stone. We talked for a while and I mentioned my boots and he said he didn't recall taking my boots. I said to him, "TK, you left me a f**king letter, saying you took my boots." He said, "I remember now" and we laughed about it. He told me he now lives in Corpus Christi, Texas for 6 months and he lives in Seattle for 6 months. He told me if I ever came to either place, he would buy me dinner and tell me what happened to my jump boots.

About two years later my wife and I visited our daughter, Donna, who was teaching in Texas, I found out we were about two hours away from Corpus Christi. So, I called him and we visited him. We stayed over night and he took us out to dinner. He told me his house in Seattle burnt down with everything in it, while he was away, including all his army stuff and my boots. He had good insurance so he was well compensated for it.

He asked me, "Do you remember when I used to tell you about my grandmother? She used to shoot rabbits on her farm in Texas and come back and cook them.

One day, my brother knocked on the door and I opened up the door and he said to me, "I sold grandma's farm for two million dollars. You get a million and I get one million." He came into the house and I signed some papers and he gave me a check for One Million Dollars $$$." Just like the television show, "The Millionaire, 1955-60. "My brother was about 5 years older than me," he said, "we never fought over anything, we just don't see one another. He left and I never saw him again."

I used to talk to TK on the phone a lot. Whenever it snowed in Philadelphia, he would call and say to me, "If you want to get out of the snow, it is only a plane ticket away to come visit me."

The Battle of Bong Trang, August 25, 1966
The Longest Day of My Life

We were out in the field for ten days. We went back into our camp and pulled guard, two hours on and four hours off.

On the morning of August 25th, Sgt. Rivera ran down and told us to grab our water and our weapons and ammunition. 'C' Company made contact with the VC. In attempting to establish a night ambush, 'C' Company set itself up in a trench, in the middle of a VC battalion base camp, but we did not know that at the time. I was about to experience the longest day of my life.

That was at daybreak. We started walking, then jogging for about twenty minutes, then tanks came by and picked us up. We climbed on the tanks. We started going through the jungle knocking down trees and bushes. It was amazing how powerful the tanks were. I was on the left side of the tank and Sgt Rivera and others were on the right side of the tank. As I was looking around the jungle, I got hit by a branch and it knocked me off the tank. When I got up, we were being mortared by the enemy. I went on the other side of the tank and Sgt Rivera was hit in the backside. His butt was all torn up with shrapnel and mortar. I asked him, "Can I help you?" He said, "No, just get the medic and tell him to come over here."

I continued running until I saw a soldier lying on the ground, moaning. I ran over to him and his eye had popped out onto his cheek, and his face was bloody. He continued moaning, "Help me, help me." I didn't recognize him; he must have been from 'C' Company. I was getting ready to drag him back to where Sgt Rivera was.

I glanced across the path and a VC was there, fifteen feet away, looking at me. He had a small carbine rifle and it looked like he was firing at me. I shot at him five times then he went down. I was going to run over to him, but I thought, let me take this wounded guy back to where Sgt Rivera was. So, I started dragging him back to Rivera. I told Rivera this guy is hurt, too. He said, "Did you get a medic"? I said, "No." It was very confusing; all I could hear was gun firing and yelling all over the place. I was going to stay with them and protect them. Sgt. Rivera said, "No, just go on."

I fired my rifle into the trees as I was running across the little field. Then I threw myself onto the ground as I was firing my rifle. When I got up to move, two VC came running out of the jungle toward me, one had a machete and the other one had a hand-made ax. I thought about running but where could I run to, they would catch up to me and kill me. I tried firing at them but my rifle was empty; so, quickly I put in another ammo clip. I looked over and shot them. They looked young, maybe 15 years old, you can't tell how old they are because they all look young. They were ready to kill me; I had no choice.

I continued moving through the jungle and I hooked up with my company. The new Lieutenant panicked and yelled, "They are surrounding us, pull back, pull back"! We pulled back and I ran into Captain Downs, he said, "What are you doing back here"? I said the Lieutenant told us to pull back. He said go back up there. I picked up another weapon and I went up but everyone was coming back. It was very confusing. Guys were screaming, yelling, and shooting, that was the last thing I remembered....

Carson, a guy from Ohio, found me lying on the ground. I didn't remember what happened right before, right after, or how I got there, and I didn't remember how long I was lying on the ground. He crawled over to me and started shaking me. He thought I was dead at first, but then he saw my leg moving. I looked up at him, I knew he was from my company. I was confused and disoriented, I couldn't hear him, and I couldn't understand what he was saying, he was talking to me, but I didn't understand. I didn't know it at the time that blood was coming from my ears because I had a perforated eardrum and I was confused because I had a concussion from the loud bombs that exploded near me. Blood was rolling down my legs from the shrapnel that hit me. I put my head back down on the ground and closed my eyes, my head was killing me. Carson crawled away.

When I opened my eyes again, I realized I was in trouble. All around us, airplanes were dropping napalm, a highly flammable sticky jelly used in incendiary bombs, consisting of gasoline thickened with special soaps. I could feel the heat of the napalm, I could see the big fire, and I could feel the ground shaking. It was very close to us.

I got my thoughts together and crawled over to Carson. He told me there was a VC bunker about twenty feet away with GIs in it and they won't let him in. We crawled over and I yelled to them, "We are coming in." My head was f**king killing me. A GI inside the bunker yelled, "No, you stay out there and watch the back, so no one comes from behind." I yelled, "What are you, f**king nuts? They are dropping napalms on us? They are killing us out here. The planes can't see where we are because the trees cover everything. If you don't let us come in, I will throw a f**king grenade in there." He then said, "Okay you can come in."

I crawled down and told Carson to come with me. They wouldn't let Carson in earlier. Then the GI in the bunker asked, "Who was the one that was going to throw a grenade in here?" I said, "Me." He grabbed me and pushed me up against the wall. I said, "We're not fighting now, I'll fight you when we get the f**k out of here. They are dropping napalms all around us, this is no time to fight each other, let's get out of here first."

All night long, airplanes dropped flare parachutes that lit up the jungle, so we could see the enemy easier.

The next morning when the sun started coming up, we could hear soldiers walking through the jungles yelling, "We are coming through, if you are in the bunkers, get out." Reinforcement was coming to help us. If we didn't get out of the bunker, they would have thrown grenades down there, thinking we were the VC.

I could see the Fourth Infantry Division coming through. The Sgt was yelling, "If you were here over night, pick up the wounded or dead and bring them back to the helicopters." Carson and I saw a wounded soldier and we carried him to a helicopter. We put him on and I jumped on too. The battle was over. The machine gunner said this helicopter is just for the wounded. I kept pointing my "thumb up" for the helicopter to take off, and they did.

They took us to a temporary field hospital in a secure area, where the doctors and nurses took care of the badly wounded first. After waiting a few hours, they stitched up my leg and cleaned my ears. The doctor said I had a concussion and punctured ear drums.

I hung around there for a day or two and stayed out of everybody's way. I went up to the mess hall, ate, and slept in the medical tent. Then a Lieutenant asked me, "Aren't you suppose to be back with your company?" I said, "Yeah, I am waiting for a helicopter." He pointed to where the helicopters land. I found the one that was going to Phouc Vinh and it flew me back.

When I landed, I had to walk about four miles back to 'B' Company. A deuce and a half passed by me with soldiers in it. I saw Tom Bommarito jump up, and he started yelling to the driver, "Let me off." He came running back to me and hugged me. He said "I thought I lost all my friends today; I am so happy to see you." We hugged and talked. I said, "It was not an easy day." We continued walking back to base camp together. We are still good friends today, and talk on the phone for hours.

I just now got off the phone talking to Tom Bommarito, he lives in Dearborn, Michigan. We were talking about Vietnam and he was giving me some details. He corrected me and said the guy's name was Carter not Johnson. Tom said when my buddy Jimmy Fogarty shot the shotgun through the roof of the tent, it was over Carter's bunk, not Johnson. Every time it rained; he would get wet.

Carter would yell and scream, "I'm going to run down there and kick Cubbage's ass." The other guys in the tent yelled back at him, "I wouldn't do that if I were you." Tommy and I laugh every time he tells me that story.

Tommy also says on August 25th his Lieutenant kept telling four GIs to 'keep moving up', then all four of them got killed. When the battle was over the Lieutenant put himself in for a medal. Tom, and a few other GIs, went up to the captain, and told him that the Lieutenant shouldn't get any medals, he didn't deserve it, he should be court-martialed for getting those four soldiers killed.

On the day they gave out medals the captain put Tom and the other GIs, who complained about the Lieutenant, on bunker duty, so they wouldn't be around to openly protest the Lieutenant getting medals, and the captain threatened them, they would get court-martialed if they did protest. I didn't know that at the time.

 I was surprised they gave me medals: a purple heart and a bronze star with a 'V' device. I didn't expect nor did I want them. I just wanted to get out of Vietnam.

I often wonder today, how did I ever survive that day, as a matter of fact, how did I ever survive, a whole year in Vietnam.

Captain Downs was wounded that day. Then they gave us a new captain, who was our old captain, Captain Lupus, the one I didn't get along with.

To our surprise on September 1st, 1966, they were going to pay us, and send us on leave for the day. We got paid in the morning and they put us on helicopters to Lock Key, a big village, which had jitneys with little drivers. The jitneys could fit three or four GIs in the back. The town had stores where you could buy clothes, eat at restaurants and bars and mamasan places. They told all the MPs to stay away and leave us alone.

Colonel Prillaman said the soldiers who were left, who did not die, needed to relieve some of the stress they were feeling after the big battle.

Young and I went into a bar and we saw Greer talking to a mamasan, who was sitting on his lap. Young picked the mamasan up, threw her over his shoulders, and carried her into a hallway that had a lot of rooms. He slammed the door and Greer couldn't tell which room Young went into. About five minutes later, Young came out of the room laughing, saying, "Here you can have her back now." He didn't do anything; we just had a big laugh.

It was a fun day, we relieved some of the stress we were feeling. Guys were riding up and down the street, having a good time on the over-crowded jitneys. We went from bar to bar just having a good time. They flew us back to Phuoc Vin, our base camp, that night.

"The Battle of Bong Trang" in My Friend's Own Words

My friend, Chuck Mundahl, 'C' company, tells in his own words, his story of the Battle of Bong Trang, the longest day and night of his young life. Chuck and I are still good friends today. He lives in Minnesota; I call him often and we see each other at reunions.

Chuck Mundahl, August 25, 1966

"My name is Chuck Mundahl, on August 25th, 1966, I was a member of reinforced 15-man patrol. Our objective was to set up an ambush at a V.C. water and resupply area. We left on the early evening of August 24th moving through fairly open terrain, in two columns, with the patrol leader, a compass, and a map. After about an hour or so the point man on the right side started to notice arrows on the ground pointing in the same direction as we were going. I was on the point on the left side. We stopped and took a look, there was no doubt someone was marking a trail. We called back to our C.O. Captain William Mullen for advice and he said proceed with caution. It was now dark and we were still not at the ambush site. Sgt. Smith was thinking we were off course so he radioed back that we were going to set up a night defensive position so as not to walk into some other ambush, and we would get to our objective in the morning.

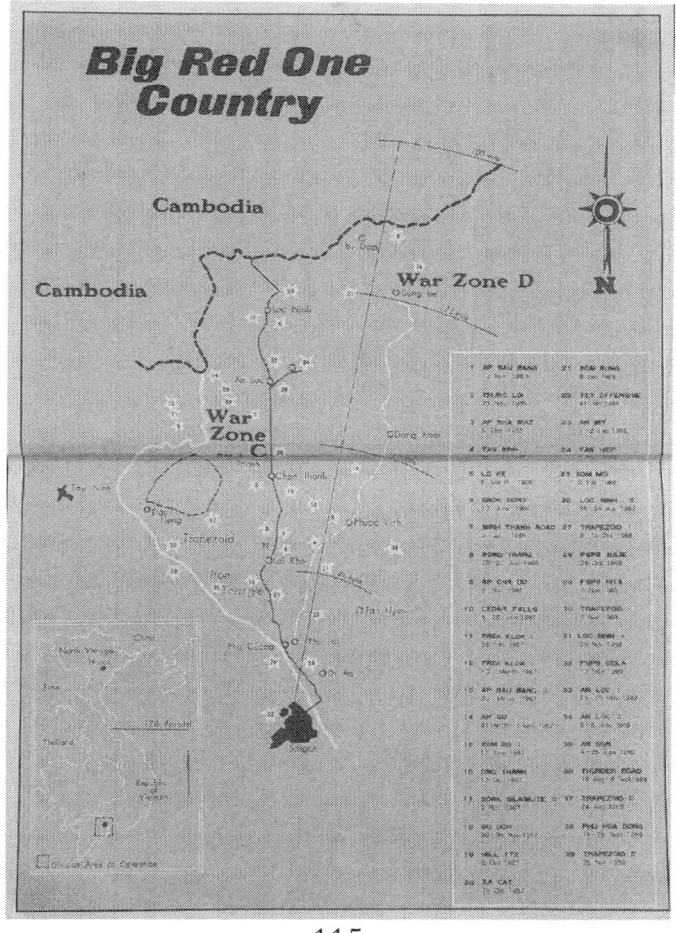

The next morning, we again started out, now we were getting into more dense jungle. We were moving in a single file and I was 2nd from the last man. We had been moving for about a half hour when we heard the point open fire and the sound of high-pitched voices, more like excited kids yelling. I'm thinking, man, are they shooting at some kids? As we, in the back of the patrol, started moving up, we noticed about 20 to 30 V.C. standing and running around. There were trenches and bunkers next to us that were empty so we took up positions there and then it got wild. We could hear Sgt. Smith yelling into the radio, "Mayday, Mayday, Mayday," they are everywhere. He made contact with Captain Mullen and told him there were 500 enemy around us. Captain Mullen told him the only way to save us would be to call artillery on top of us. This is what he did. It felt like my body was going to split in half. They backed off for a moment. Word came up the line to "Hang tough."

Captain Mullen was coming with the rest of our Company C and B Company, 1st BN 2nd Inf, 1st Inf. Div. and the 1-4th Cav. It didn't take the enemy long to get organized. They started to surround us and we began to take on heavy casualties. Grenades were flying, along with automatic weapon fire on both sides. At that point, a grenade exploded just above my head. I was blown back, contents were blown out of my pockets, as were my helmet and glasses. My left shoulder and ankle and inner left thigh were burning and it felt like I had been kicked in the groin. We now are several dead and wounded. We could hear tanks and PCs from the 1-4 in the distance. Smith passed the word and he and his radioman and another man were going to get help. They got up and all three were hit by the enemy claymore. Sgt Smith and the radioman were both killed and another man had badly wounded legs, but we found out he later crawled to a clearing and a gunship spotted him and came down and picked him up. The calvary was now getting closer, and then all hell broke loose, as they hit the enemy line. There was enemy mortar, heavy machine gun fire, artillery and air support fire. The noise was deafening. There were now 8 dead and 5 wounded, 1 man not wounded. We crawled into an empty enemy bunker. Through the firing slots of the bunker we could see the VC outside. We would fire at them. They tried to finish us off by tossing grenades into the bunker from their trench. By now the cav. and C-1-2 were taking their interest, and they were reorganizing again. They must have thought we were all dead. We had very little water left and it went fast. I went through my pack and opened cans of fruit and passed them around. The heat was getting bad, this bunker was built for Vietnamese not Americans. Outside the fight was raging, inside we didn't know what else was in store for us.

As the day started toward evening and soon it started getting dark and quiet. We started to whisper about what our next move should be. I thought for sure they would bomb the hell out of the place, but a night move was not going to work. What turned out to be the longest day of our young lives, was coming to an end.

As the sun came up the guy who wasn't wounded said, "Let's go," so, we crawled out. He told me and another guy to move out about 20 meters and wait for the rest. While we waited, two VC came along. I had a grenade, he had a M16, my rifle jammed. My buddy was taking aim. I used hand signals to tell him to hold off. This could be the point men of a larger group. They passed us and the others. The two VC went right between us. After they passed, we got up and moved ahead. I could see a clearing and I noticed the white from a star on an APC. I waved to my buddy to come my way. As I could see the gunner behind the 50cal machine gun, I began yelling don't shoot, as we went hopping toward our line.

Soon medics grabbed us and a Sgt, from our Co. came over to see what was going on. He couldn't believe we were still alive. They got the rest of the guys out of the bunker.

I have had many sleepless nights thinking about that day and the guys who didn't make it. I still pray for them. Chuck Mundahl, Co, C 1st Bn. 2nd. Inf, 1st Inf. Div.

This patrol caused the battle of Bong Trang. We never knew the battle as **Bong Trang**, but as the **Battle of Aug, 25th**.

When I see Chuck at our reunions in Pigeon Forge, Tennessee, I tease him and say, "You are one of the guys who almost got me killed." He laughs and replies. "I almost got myself killed, let alone getting you killed."

Worthless Fat Sergeant

About a week after August 25^{th,} we started getting new soldiers in our company, Livingston and Dawson, and I can't remember the other guys' names. For some reason they transferred a fat sergeant, who was a cook, to our company. We already had a cook; so, they made him our squad leader. When he went out on patrol with us, he was worthless. The first time he faked heat exhaustion. We had to wait for an hour and half until he could get up and continue walking.

The second time he went out on patrol with us he faked a heart attack and he fell down. The Lieutenant made us carry him on a poncho liner. Greer, Young and I started dragging him on the ground. We were hitting stumps and rocks, then he got up. He got upset with us because he wasn't being carried carefully. Guys in our squad got into an argument with him. When we went back to base camp the Lieutenant said we should have some respect for the sergeant.

When we were out on ambush patrol, he would sleep instead of pulling guard. He never did his share. He wouldn't dig any fox holes, but he would want to jump into the fox hole if we made contact with the enemy. The guys told him they were going to shoot him, if he tried to jump into their fox holes.

One night we were supposed to go out on ambush patrol and one of the guys in our squad said, "No, we are not going out with that fat sergeant." We all agreed we weren't going out with him again. The lieutenant said we had to go out or I will court-martial you for refusing a direct order. We told him we are not going out with him because he was worthless.

The lieutenant went up and got the sergeant major. He was a Korean War Veteran; he was in his forties. He came down and said, "You are all going out on patrol with the sergeant." Then he grabbed one guy from New York and started shaking him and calling him a coward. They started punching one another and rolling on the ground. We just stood there and let them fight. The kid from New York was really doing a job on the Sergeant Major. The Lieutenant came running down and broke it up. We did not go out that night. The kid from New York was transferred the next day, and I never knew what happened to him.

We heard the captain didn't want to get involved with this incident because he did not know what to do with the seven of us. About a week later the fat sergeant got transferred out. We don't know what happened to him either.

Years later, at a First Infantry reunion, I was at a table and, an old guy that I did not recognize, told me he was the first sergeant of B Company. Then I told him my name, but he said he didn't remember me. I said, "But I remember you, I saw you get your ass kicked." He said, "I remember that, I shouldn't have grabbed the GI." I asked what happened to him? He said, "I don't remember what happened to him." Then I told him it was all about that worthless fat sergeant. We got along well at the reunion; the last I heard, he was pretty sick.

A Visit from My Friend, "The Fogue Guy"

September, 1966 I was sleeping in my tent in Phuoc Vin, when Jimmy Fogarty, came to visit me. He had a two-day pass to come over to see me. He was in the 173rd airborne. We weren't in Phuoc Vin a lot, we spent most of our time out in the jungles, but this day we happened to be there. He shook me, to wake me up, and I said, "Hi, Jim" and I rolled over and went back to sleep. He shook me again and then I realized it was the "Fogue Guy." I immediately got up. I said, "Let's go to Phuoc Vinh and we'll have a couple of beers together." I gave him a M16 rifle and I grabbed my M16 rifle. Jimmy asked, "Are you allowed to take rifles into town?" I said, "Yeah, they don't call it Dodge City for nothing."

We went into town and we were having a few drinks and talking. There were other GIs in the bar too. The bar was pretty full. A sniper started shooting at our table and at the bar. Then we all shot back at the sniper, on the roof-top, across the street. The sniper fell off the roof of the beer-can wall building. I didn't have a pass, so I said we better get out of here before the MPs come and start asking questions. We went back to our base camp and had a few more beers.

Then I said, "Let's go meet a friend of mine, Tommy Bommarito, he is in another platoon." We went into his tent; he was playing cards with about four guys. He was happy to see us. We sat down on a bunk.

A black soldier, by the name of Carter, came walking back into the tent. He didn't like me from a previous incident we had in a bar. Some of the black guys told me, there were two or three brothers, who were still mad at me for coming into their black only bar, with my M-16 rifle with another white guy.

Carter yelled at Fogarty, "You get off my f**king bed." I got up and punched Carter and he fell across two bunks. He ran out of the tent and came back in with a machine gun, a M60. I said to Fogue, "Let's get the hell out of here." Guys grabbed the machine gun from Carter, and we ran out of the tent.

We went back to my tent and we drank a few more beers. I began thinking, "Who the hell do they think they are, chasing us out of their tent? I said, "Here Fogue, here's a shot gun." He looked at it and put two rounds in it. I grabbed my M16 rifle. I said, "Let's go back to the tent." He asked, "What are we going to do?" I said "We are going to surround them." It seemed like a good idea; I was a little drunk at the time. I said, "You go in the front way, and I'll go around the back way. We'll surround them." Fogue says, "That sounds like a good idea."

It had been over an hour since we were last in there. They were all drinking and smoking, playing Motown records, like the Temptations, singing and dancing and having a good old time. They didn't notice us when we came back into the tent. We yelled, "Hey, we are back." They weren't listening to us; they didn't even notice us walk into the tent with our rifles. Fogue decided to shoot two holes in the roof of the tent to get their attention…that stopped everything...he got their attention. I didn't realize what he was going to do, I was surprised too.

Everyone started arguing with each other. Bird said to me, "We can settle this, this guy, Carter, wants to fight you, put your gun down and let's all go outside."

Carter and I, along with everyone else, went out of the tent and we started fighting, punching and rolling on the ground. I was drunk. Young, another black guy, who was in my squad, and on my machine gun crew, pulled Carter off of me and started fighting him. Some of the black guys did not like the idea that one black guy would defend a white guy, over another black guy. Then another black guy came outside with a machine gun, and he wanted to shoot us.

Fogue and I ran away, outside the perimeter. I said, "The guys are looking for us, they have their guns, and we don't have any weapons with us... so, we might as well go to sleep here, out in the field."

When we woke up in the morning, Fogue said, "What are we going to do?" I said, "We are going up to the mess hall." If anyone starts any shit, we'll start punching them. There will be officers there and they might have four, but not twenty guys, from last night, and they won't have their rifles or machine guns with them."

When we walked up to the mess hall, the guys from the night before were waving to us, from the mess hall line. They said, "You are one crazy mother f**kers, you guys are really crazy. That was one crazy night last night. None of the officers found out, and we're keeping quiet about it, nobody is gonna say nuffin."

Fogarty said, "I don't believe this, this is one crazy outfit." We had breakfast together and Fogue said, "I'm getting out of here! I am going back to my 173rd.

"We hugged one another, and he said, ... "I'll see you back in Philly."

I Visit my Friend, "The Fogue Guy" in Bien Hoa

In November, 1966, about two months later, I told the captain, I never had an in-country R&R (rest & recuperation). You get one in-country R&R, and one out-of-country R&R. I went to Hong Kong for my out-of-country R&R.

He gave me a five-day pass. I went down to the airfield and I told them I want to go to Bien Hoa, the 173rd air base near Saigon. I knew what unit my friend, Jimmy Fogarty, was in and I tracked Fogue down. A truck took me down there. I ate at his mess hall. All those guys were air-borne. They would get up in the morning, do drills and march.

We never did any of that in our outfit. We were a rag-tag outfit. We never did any exercises, PT or marching. They never had any control over us. It was just as dangerous in our base camp, as it was out in the field.

I laughed when he went out for PT, what a difference between his camp and my camp. Fogue took me to his supply tent, and he gave me new jungle boots, new fatigues, new poncho liner and a new backpack. Our outfit had the Old-World War II backpacks. The one he gave me was a new, aluminum backpack.

We had a nice visit. As I was leaving, I said, "I'll see you back in the world."

I was the only one in my battalion who had an aluminum backpack. The guys would ask me, "Where did you get your backpack?" I said, "The supply sergeant gave it to me." Guys went down and asked for a new backpack but our supply sergeant said he doesn't have any new ones. They couldn't figure out where I got it. One guy said, "I would steal it from you, but being that you are the only one who has one, you would know that I was the one who took it."

The Tunnel

One time, a Lieutenant from West Point, I don't remember his name, took over our platoon. He said, "I am from West Point and I know you guys have seen a lot of action but I wouldn't ask you to do anything, I wouldn't do." We had about 25 guys left in our platoon, usually a platoon had 40 guys. He gave us a nice little talk. He seemed pretty good at the time. He went out on patrols with us. He sort of listened to us when we were on ambush patrols.

Once, we came into a deserted base camp where we found a tunnel, the Lieutenant called in to the captain and told him what we found. The captain told him, have someone go into the tunnel and see what is down there. He turned around and asked who is volunteering to go down into the tunnel? All of us knew we were not going to be a tunnel rat or anything like that. He said, "I need a volunteer." No one said anything, He said, "If no one volunteers I am going to appoint one of you." No one said anything. He started looking at each guy, one by one. The guys started looking down on the ground and turning their heads, they did not want to make eye contact with him.

He looked at me and I looked at him. I said, "Didn't you say, when you first came here, you wouldn't ask anyone to do something that you wouldn't do?" He said. "Shut up, Cubbage" I said, "I am not shutting up, and I am not going the f**k down there." One of the newer guys volunteered to go down. He went down the tunnel and he did not find anything there. The Lieutenant was annoyed with me, we never got along after that. A little while later the Lieutenant took me to the side and told me never to talk that way to him in front of the men. This incident happened after the big battle on August 25th.

"We Are in a Hostile Area"

Another time we were out in the field and our company was cutting the elephant grass down to make a landing field for helicopters. The sergeant said to me, and Young, and Greer, "I have a good detail for you." We went down about a mile to a rice patty. He said, "While we are cutting down the elephant grass, make sure no one comes across the rice paddies, so we don't get hit." We set up the machine gun and we started cooking our sea rations and eating and having a pretty good time. We could see for miles over the rice paddies.

The second day we are out there with our fatigues off, making coffee and having a good time. A helicopter flies over and comes back around again and started to come down and land on the side where we were. I said, "Didn't they see that landing field that they are cutting down about a mile up the road, maybe they are lost? What the hell are they doing?"

A little guy got out, and we walked over to the helicopter. He said with a southern drawl, "Do you know you are in a **hostile country**?" We looked at one another and laughed and I thought to myself "Yeah... we know we are in **hostile country**; they are trying to kill us here." He said, "Don't you see my rank, I am a major, you should salute me." I thought to myself, "We don't salute officers in the field because we are in a **hostile area"** I said to myself, "F**k you" and I saluted him and so did Greer and Young. The major said, "Put your fatigues and helmet on, and one of you soldiers get behind the machine gun in case the enemy comes through the rice paddies."

We had a clear view of the field, it would take the VC at least an hour to walk through the rice paddies, which was bigger than a football field. We put our helmets and fatigues back on and Greer got behind the machine gun. The major turned around and went back to his helicopter. As he started flying up, Young said to me, "Let's salute him, maybe the VC will see us saluting him, and they will know he is an officer, and they might think he is important, and shoot him the f**k down." I said, "Greer, come on over, we'll all salute him together, as he flies away."

Two hours later the sergeant came up with three other soldiers, and he told us, we are being replaced. The major said he didn't like the way we were pulling guard duty. I told him, "You were the best guys I have. I don't know what the f**k you did, but he wasn't happy with you, and he wanted you replaced."

Young and Greer and I would often laugh about it, repeating his words with a southern drawl, "Don't you know you are in a **hostile area**"? "Of course, we know we are in a hostile area, you idiot, **they are trying to kill us here.**" We laughed about that all year long. Whenever we saw each other, we would laugh and say "**Brother, don't you know you are in a hostile area.**" I always thought he was the biggest idiot in the world. I wish I could remember the major's name.

The Big Dust Off

Less than a week later, the same major, the biggest idiot in the world, wanted to see how rugged we were.

We were only allowed to have a half canteen of water and then we started sweeping through the jungle about 8:00 am during the hot and dry season. It didn't rain for months then. The temperature got up to 105 degrees. As we were walking through the jungle at about 12 noon soldiers were beginning to fall out from heat exhaustion. We picked them up and tried to help the guys. I was exhausted. I met up with Tommy Bommarito and I said to him, "Let's fall out" (just lay down). We were so thirsty and tired, we couldn't walk anymore. We laid down with a lot of other guys. I thought to myself, "If the enemy came now, they could kill us and the whole company, because we were too exhausted to fight back." Afterwards, they put us on helicopters and flew us around for ten minutes, to help bring our body temperature down. Then they put other soldiers on helicopters to cool them down.

We went back to base camp later that day and when Colonel Prillaman returned, and he heard about the incident, he had the major replaced. That Major only lasted about ten days. We often laughed about him. I only wish I knew his name; he was there for such a short time, no one could remember his name. This was known as "The Big Dust Off."

There were a lot of officers who didn't last very long, for one reason or the other.

No Bob Hope Show, December, 1966

We came back into Phuoc Vinh, our base camp, around December 18, 1966. They said we were going to stay in base camp until after New Year's.

I went out one night to the EM Club and I ran into the cook, Whitaker, from Philly, and we decided to walk back to our tents and we walked by the officer's EM Club (Enlisted Men's Club). He said, "Let's stop in here and have a drink." I said, "We can't go in here, that is the officer's club. They won't serve us." He said, "Let's go in and say we are officers and we just came in from out in the jungles." We went inside and we ordered two beers. There was a sergeant behind the bar and he said, "You are not officers, we can't serve you." Then he said, "I'll serve you one beer, the officers will not like it when they find out you are not one of them." So, we bought the beer and talked to the sergeant until we finished the beer. He said, "I can't give you another one." So, we left.

When we waked outside the MPs pulled up in a jeep, they walked past us and they went into the Officer's Club. As we got closer to their jeep, Whitaker said, "Let's take it. I can drive a jeep." I jumped in it. He started driving down the road with no lights. He couldn't find the light switch on the jeep. But he kept driving because we wanted to get out of the area. We didn't want the MPs to see us. It was pitch black out. He missed the turn in the road and he went down an embankment. He hit the barbed wire and I flew out and over the hood of the jeep and hit the ground.

Just then a helicopter came down with their search lights on us. I started waving to them yelling, "Don't shoot we are American soldiers, don't shoot" I could see him telling the pilot something, that's how close he was to us. Then they flew away. Whitaker helped me up. We had to get out of the area fast. My leg was killing me, I was in pain. We made it to my tent, about 4 miles away, on a sore leg. Whitaker got me a bucket of ice so I could ice it all night.

The next morning a lot of guys were going to Camranh Bay to see Bob Hope and the Christmas show. Two friends, Greer and Young, my machine gun crew, said they would carry me. I didn't want to go to sick call because I was afraid, they would ask me how I hurt my knee. They would probably figure out someone must have gotten hurt in that stolen jeep when it went over the embankment.

So, I stayed in my tent all day and I missed the Bob Hope Show. For the next couple of days, I iced my knee and I couldn't walk. We didn't go out on patrol until after New Year's.

The German Shepherd

January, 1967 When we were out on an operation, I don't remember which operation, a new soldier joined us and he had a German Shepherd with him. They told us the dog will be able to smell and detect the Viet Cong before we do, and it will save us from being killed or wounded. They put him with our squad to go out on an ambush patrol. The dog started jumping around. The handler said, "There are Viet Cong out there." The handler was doing something to the dog to make him jump and growl, but we weren't sure what it was. We pulled back, and went back to our base camp. We told the Lieutenant that the Viet Cong were out there. They ordered us to open fire and shoot into the jungle. We stayed up all night waiting for the Viet Cong to attack, nothing happened. The next morning the whole company went out and swept the area. We couldn't find any sign that anyone was ever out there. That happened two or three times when we went out with the

German Shepherd and its handler. The captain sent them to another platoon.

It was, my friend, Sergeant Richard "Bird" Glenn's squad. They went out on an ambush patrol and the dog started jumping around again. The handler told the soldiers that the VC were out there in the jungle, so the guys in the squad started shooting.

Sergeant Richard Glenn went back to base camp and told the captain, "The handler said his dog was jumping around because he can smell VC there in the jungles, so we started shooting." Then they realized the dog wasn't with them. Captain Lupus accused Sergeant Glenn of shooting the dog. He said, "I didn't shoot the dog." They were going to give Sergeant Glenn an article 15.

The next morning the company went back out into the jungle and found the dead dog. It was shot by a .45 hand gun. The only one who had a .45 was the handler. The handler finally admitted that the dog jumped in front of him. All of us in our squad thought that the handler shot his dog because we were in a bad area, and we were making contact with a lot of VC, and he didn't want to go out anymore. They told us he was sent back to train with another dog.

Of the 4,000 dogs that served in Vietnam, fewer than 200 made it back to the states. Not a pleasant thought to consider given their incredible devotion to duty. I've heard it said that without our military dogs, there would be 10,000 additional names on the Vietnam Veterans Memorial Wall.

I'm Short

On February 2, 1967 I was getting 'short' which means I was getting ready to leave. When you have about a month left in Vietnam, GIs would yell, "I'm short, I'm so short they think I am a midget." Which means I don't have much time left in the country.

We were out on an operation and I knew that by February 11, my birthday, I should be back at base camp to get ready to leave for home. We dug a fox hole for the night and I blew up an air mattress to sleep on. I was the gunner but I gave Young the job of being the machine gunner and I carried the ammunition and my M16. We put the flares and the claymore mines in front of us. We haven't had any contact with the VC for weeks. We pulled guard when it got dark. I went to sleep on my air mattress outside the fox hole.

Around midnight, mortars started coming in towards us, blowing up, sixty feet away from us. I rolled off the mattress and in the dark, I thought I was crawling towards the fox hole but I was crawling away from it. Then came another explosion about 40 feet away. I could hear Young and Greer yelling to me, "Hey Cubbage, you're going the wrong way, you better come back here, or you're going to get your ass killed." I looked around and I saw a flash and then I could see their heads. I turned around and quickly started crawling back to them in the fox hole. They were laughing and said, "You didn't know which way to go, you were crawling the wrong way."

The Viet Cong would sometimes shoot four or five mortars and then take off deeper into the jungle, and leave before we could figure out where they were.

We stayed out in the jungle on this operation until February 14. Then we went back to our base camp, Phuoc Vinh.

We were in base camp for two days when they told our squad that we had to go out again on ambush patrol. As I came closer to my expected departure date, I withdrew myself from battle, I was determined I was not going out again, I wanted to survive and return home safely.

I was on my bunker with my shirt off, working on a nice tan to go back home to Philly. I said to the guys, "I am short, I am going home in 7 or 8 days. I am not going out on patrol" The sergeant came down and said, "You have to go out with your squad on ambush patrol." I said, "No, I am too short to go out. I heard many stories about guys who went out on their last patrol and got killed. I am not going out."

They brought down my friend, Tommy Bommarito, who was a sergeant then. He said, "I'll go out with you, Ed." I said "No, Tom, f**k you, and that sergeant with you. I am not going out on ambush patrol." Tom ran back to tell the captain. Captain Lupus agreed and said, "He's not going out, he saw enough fighting, and I don't blame him." Tom came back and said, "The captain said you are restricted to your bunker, until you leave the country. Only come up to the mess hall to eat." I said, "That's fine with me."

997 were killed their first day

1,448 were killed on their last day

Time to Go Home

I left Vietnam on February 22, 1967, Tommy and I came in together, and we left together. We were the only two who survived, out of about 10 guys, who came in with us, back on February 22, 1966.

A helicopter flew us back to Camp Alpha, the place we landed one year ago, when we first came to Vietnam. Sgt. Tom Bommarito left to go home on the first plane. You boarded the plane by rank when you left to go home.

It would be another 2 or 3 hours before they'd call another group of guys to board the plane, so I went down to the EM Club. They were playing the same songs, that they played, when we first flew into Vietnam, every other song was, the Green Beret.

I ordered a beer in the EM Club, and a guy turned around and said to me, "Yo, Cubbage, I heard you were killed." I looked at him and it was Howie. The guy I got into a fight for, with a big Samoan in Hawaii, on our way to Vietnam. Howie lost his $20 to a palm reader and I was going to get it back for him. I said, "No, I wasn't killed." Howie said, "I knew you weren't killed. If you didn't get killed that night by the big Samoan when he punched you, and you fell out into the street, and almost got hit by a car, I knew you would not get killed in Nam."

He asked me, "How did you ever make it out of here alive?" I said, "I don't know." I said, "How about you?" He said, "I don't know either." We just wanted to survive our year in-country and go home.

He was in the 173rd Airborne, where I was supposed to go. We talked for about an hour, then they called our names to board the plane. I didn't sit near him on the plane. I'm sorry I didn't get his phone number when we left.

We all started cheering and yelling on the plane as we flew up and away from Vietnam.

When we landed in California, a sergeant, who had a CIB on his fatigues, came onto the plane. He yelled to all of us, "Do you guys want to go home? In the airport protestors will by yelling at you, saying you are baby killers, and they want the war to stop. If you fight with them, they will lock you up, and them too. They will get a free meal, which they probably want. Don't say anything to them, just go home." We left the airport, among screaming protestors, without saying a word.

No Welcome Home Parade for Our Vietnam War Veterans

Vietnam War Veterans were not given the hero status, that they gave to the returning soldiers from WWII. Most boys were 18-year-olds, fresh out of high school. We were courageous boys who loved our country by performing our patriotic duty. We were doing what Uncle Sam needed us to do, and we were proud to have the opportunity to serve our country. We answered our nation's call. We served with honor and distinction.

No welcome home parades for our Vietnam Vets partly due to the logistics of the never-ending conflict. We usually came home one at a time. The Vietnam War lasted from **1959-1975, sixteen years**, the longest war in American history, at that time.

We were sent back home with no readjustment to the lifestyle in the states, which had changed dramatically in one year. No deprogramming of what you learned from the military. You find there's no one you can talk to or who can understand what you've been through, not even your family. After I came home from Vietnam, my life saving grace was getting away from it all, and taking a trip across the country in my 1950 New York Chrysler with my friend Ed Collins.

Freedom Is Not Free

The bravery of our Vietnam Vets during and after this war is unparalleled to any war in our history. We put our lives on the line every day for our nation. We sacrificed long days and hot tiring, dirty nights, tasteless food and crowded bunks and endless fights.

Running into battle when it would have been easier to walk away.

Freedom is not free, many of my friends paid the ultimate sacrifice. We are forever indebted to our soldiers. In the last few years, we are finally getting recognized for our sacrifices we made so many years ago.

Thank You for Your Service

I would like to thank Matthew Rocco of "**The Semper Fi Fund, LCpl Parsons Welcome Home Fund**" whose mission is to care for veterans from all military service branches who were wounded from combat operations in Vietnam. They have helped Vietnam Veterans with mortgages, utilities, rent, repair, and home modifications. They even sent us chicken soup and hams during the pandemic to encourage us to stay home and stay safe. Thank you for caring when so many did not, 50 years ago.

Thank you to the "**Honor Flight of Southern N.J., Pam & Ron Pontano.** They recognize American veterans for their sacrifices and achievements by taking us in parade fashion; firemen, policemen, high school students and civilians saluted us, and stopped traffic, all along the way to Washington DC. to visit the Vietnam Memorial. It was a very emotional day for us.

Thank you to the **Gloucester County Library System** for sponsoring a Veterans Oral History Project by videotaping Vietnam Veterans' experiences in Vietnam. After viewing my video, my wife encouraged me to write this book. She enjoyed hearing my stories and I gained the confidence that maybe, I could write a book.

Just a personal note, **be careful,** who you donate your money to. A lot of Veterans' Organizations collect money that is donated to them but only a small percentage goes to the Veterans. Most of their money goes to the CEO and their expenses and they call it a non-profit organization. Always google the organization first, before donating, and ask how much of the money goes directly to the veterans. Thank you.

Some Facts about the Vietnam War

- 2.91% of Vietnam War Veterans actually saw combat. The door gunner on a Vietnam era Huey gunship had a life-span of 5 minutes. The United States sent 2,796,000 soldiers to

Vietnam, 58,479 died, 300,000 were wounded, 75,000 were left severely disabled.
- January 27, 1973 President Nixon signed a Paris Peace Accord ending direct involvement in the Vietnam War. But as U.S. troops departed Vietnam, North Vietnam military officials plotted to overtake South Vietnam, and they did in 1975.
- The USA became involved in Vietnam because it feared the spread of communism. China had become communist in 1949 and communists were in control of North Vietnam. The USA was afraid that communism would spread to South Vietnam and then to the rest of Asia. It decided to send money, supplies and military advisers to help the South Vietnamese Government.
- The North Vietnamese argued they were fighting a patriotic war to rid themselves of foreign aggressors.
- The USA were unable to defeat the Vietcong and were met with growing opposition to the war back home. Opposition to the war in the United States bitterly divided Americans, even after President Nixon ordered the withdrawal of U.S. forces in 1973.

- The Vietnam War was a long, costly and divisive conflict that pitted the communist government of North Vietnam against South Vietnam and its principal ally the US. The conflict was intensified by the ongoing Cold War between US and the Soviet Union. Communist forces ended the war by seizing control of South Vietnam in 1975, and the country was unified as the Socialist Republic of Vietnam in 1976.
- No formal declaration of war was ever made, a violation of the US Constitution. Nixon cited his power as commander-in-chief of U.S. forces, under Article Two of the United States Constitution, as legal authority for operations in Vietnam.
- The US could have never won the Vietnam War, the South Vietnamese government completely lacked the leadership among the people to even build sufficient popular support and the fact that the South Vietnamese were purely reliant upon the support of the US.
- The Viet Cong fought a guerilla war, ambushing US patrols, setting booby traps and landmines, and planting bombs in towns.

They mingled in with the peasants, wearing ordinary clothes. The Americans couldn't identify who the enemy was. It was difficult for American troops to know who was a Vietcong and who was not.
- They were supplied with rockets and weapons by China and Russia.
- The American soldiers referred to the Viet Cong as Charlie.
- The Vietcong won the hearts and minds of the South Vietnamese peasants. They would offer to help them in their daily work and also promised them land, more wealth and freedom under Ho Chi Minh and the communists.

Honor Flight: (left to right: Tom Tumelty, Frank LaBletta, Dennis Egan, Edmond Cubbage, and Tracy-Elizabeth Cubbage Stoehr.) Honor Flight recognizes American veterans for their sacrifices and achievements by taking you, by bus, to Washington DC to see the Vietnam Memorial for no cost. Guardians in blue, went with us to provide assistance. Policemen, firemen, civilians and high school students stopped traffic and stood on the side and saluted us, county by county, state by state, all the way to Washington, DC.

Getting Closer to Home

After we got off the plane we got on a bus and it took us to Oakland Army Base Camp in the San Francisco Bay Area of California. I remember sitting next to a soldier and he said to me, "That is the Golden Gate Bridge. It is one of the "Seven Wonders of the Modern World" and one of the world's most beautiful bridges. It is named Golden Gate because it is the entrance to the San Francisco Bay from the Pacific Ocean.

We got off the bus and went into a big room at the Oakland Army Base. A Spec 4 gave us an orientation about what we are going to do and when we are going home. We will spend the night there, get our dress clothes, get paid, and we can go home tomorrow. I recognized the Spec 4's face from my Swampoodle neighborhood, he was from Corpus Christi parish. After the orientation I went up to him and said you are from my neighborhood, Swampoodle. He said yes, he was. He walked Howie and I up to the mess hall and told the cook to take care of us. It was the first time I ever had a T-bone steak and eggs for breakfast. We went over to the supply building and they issued us Class A uniforms, which was short sleeve khakis. It was summer in California in February, but it was winter back in Philadelphia. We got our clothes and pay, then they sent us home for a fifteen-day leave.

Finally, Home Sweet Home

They took us to the airport and I flew home to Philly. I took a yellow cab to my old Swampoodle neighborhood. I knew my parents moved but I lost the address. I asked a couple of neighbors but they did not know where they moved to.

I got on the bus and subway. I was in uniform and no one spoke to me on the bus or subway, no one said hi, no one was friendly, they just looked at me.

I was freezing and shivering, in my short sleeve shirt. Uncle Sam did not issue me a coat, it was about 37 degrees in Philadelphia. To make matters worse, my blood was thin because I had just spent a year in the tropical weather of Vietnam. But I had a nice tan, though! It ran through my mind that I made it out of Vietnam alive, after a year, but I will probably freeze to death here!

I went to my sister-in-law's, Aunt Ron's house, around Broad and Erie Avenues, a nice old lady who used to write to me in Vietnam. Aunt Ron and my mother were the only ones who wrote to me while I was in Vietnam. She made a big fuss over me and gave me milk and cookies, the best I ever tasted.

She called my brother, Tommy, and he picked me up in his car and he took me to my mother and father's new apartment, 740 Vernon Road, Stenton Hall Apartments in Mount Airy. My Mom knew I was coming home, but she did not know when. She was very happy to see me, she cried and hugged me.

Horn and Hardart

About a week later my mom told me she has a friend who wanted to sell me her car. Her friend was Mrs. Horn from Horn and Hardart. My mom said to me,

"Did you ever hear of an old lady who had a car and only drove it back and forth to Church, well she only drove it back and forth to her country club. She has an old car she wants to sell you. Don't argue with her, about the price, just give her what she wants for the car." My mom introduced her to me and she left us alone.

Mrs. Horn asked me, "You just came home from Vietnam? I watch it on television every night. I want to sell you my car." She said, "Give me a dollar." I gave her a dollar and then she gave me the keys and the title to her car. She told me to get the title changed, she had already signed it.

Horn and Hardart was a food services company in the United States noted for operating the first food service automats in Philadelphia and New York.

It was a 1950 New York Chrysler. It had fluid drive, which meant you could drive with a stick shift, or put it in automatic. It was a nice, big. black car. I drove it back and forth to Fort Dix. When I got out of the service, I took a much-needed trip across the country with a friend of mine, Ed Collins, in my black, 1950, New York Chrysler. Thank you, Mrs. Horn.

I Met the Love of My Life, in Margate, New Jersey the day Neil Armstrong landed on the moon, Sunday, July 20, 1969

A couple of years later, after all my friends got out of the service: Fogue, Ozzie, Bruno, Florida (Jim McWhorter), Frank LaBletta, Dennis Egan, Michael Egan and my brother Patrick Cubbage and other friends, started hanging out in Margate, New Jersey.

After the second year of going to Margate, I met a gorgeous blonde, named Elaine Hennessy, a Catholic School teacher from Philadelphia. We started dating and two years later we were married.

We Were Married on July 10, 1971

We Are Grateful, Thankful, and Blessed with Three Beautiful Children

Edmond John JR. is married to Donna Amit-Cubbage, an amazing teacher, and he is a teacher at Bensalem High School and the Head Football Coach. He has three gorgeous children, Aiden, 15, Princess Grace, 13, and Dillon 6.

Tracy Elizabeth is married to Steven Stoehr, and they are both successful lawyers. They have a handsome son named, Ryan, 13.

Donna Elaine is married to Howie Pollard, a dedicated husband and father. She is a teacher, and they have two beautiful princesses, Lainey, 7 and Olivia, 5.

"Our children are our rainbow in life but our grandchildren are our pot of gold."

We will be celebrating our **50th wedding anniversary in Hawaii** with all our children and grandchildren for the whole month of July, 2021.

I felt I had a good life. My friends who died in Vietnam did not have that chance.

Our loving Cubbage, Stoehr and Pollard Family!

Freedom is not free; our freedom was paid for by my friends.

Before closing, I would like to share with you a brief summary of the effects of the Viet Nam War on my dear friend, who calls me, his brother from a different mother, Joseph Michael Egan, just another kid from Swampoodle.

Effects of the Vietnam War on Joseph M. Egan

January, 1969, myself and five other guys from my neighborhood and high school, "Father Judge" volunteered for the draft. On March 10, 1969, we were inducted in the US Army. We all believed that America needed us and it was our honor to serve our country. As we departed from Basic Training, we were split up into different units. They told us that Philly guys were too crazy to be together. We all experienced combat, only four of the six, returned home wounded. Our neighborhood was devastated over the losses they suffered because two young men died and four of us were wounded. One of the young men that came home, died fifteen years later due to possible herbicides. The claim is that the cancer developed from chemicals dropped in the jungle leaving only three buddies. We were all close buddies before the war but once home we were constant reminders to each other of the pain and memories of the war which caused us to split up and go our separate ways. Very soon after my return from the war the flashbacks, the dreams, and the nightmares started to occur. I thought about the war every single day and I still do. I felt responsible for my buddies, as it was my idea to volunteer our draft. Because I was the youngest, I insisted they wait for me until I was eighteen years old, which they did. I tried college for a while then my girlfriend became pregnant so I quit school, and was married. I found a job selling insurance and was able to live life suppressing these memories and emotions the best I could. However, very soon after that, the flashbacks, bad dreams and nightmares hounded me often. I thought about the war more intensely every

single day. Consequently, this marriage ended in a divorce.

As the induction process began, I was selected for officer's candidate school but I volunteered for the infantry instead. However, the Army assigned me to Artillery School. I learned to read maps and radio techniques along with survey skills. Upon graduation, I was assigned stateside as the rest of my original buddies were all deployed to Vietnam. So, I volunteered for Vietnam as well. Soon after I arrived in Viet Nam and was assigned to a support unit. I then volunteered again to be in the field with the infantry as a radio operator assigned with the First Armored Calvary.

On May 12, 1970, I was wounded in a tank that was hit by a large RPG (rocket). I was severely burned with 2nd and 3rd degree burns on my back, buttocks and legs, with shrapnel in my legs, groin, back and face. I was sent to intensive care and burn center and rehabilitation because it was difficult walking again. After 3 months, I was released, sent to a rear support for a rest and allocated time, before my discharge papers finally arrived.

Thank you, Michael, for your story. We are sorry for the pain you and so many others went through.

Everyone who served in Vietnam has a story. That's why we go to meetings and reunions, to share our stories, and they understand.

We have a second chance in life. We honor our friends, our heroes, who made the ultimate sacrifice, by being good men and by leading a good life in their memory.

Hall of Honor

These are the soldiers who were killed the year I was in Vietnam

1966-1967

in "B" Company and "C" Company

A lot of these soldiers were good friends of mine.

May They Rest in Peace

Company "B"
Company "C"

Capt. George S. Costello	Sfc Billy A. Thompson
SSg Charles De Jean III	SSg Adrian J. Anglim
SSg Lewis J. Jackson	SSg Allen Brackins
SSg Edwin H. Levering	SSg Fortune Smith
Sgt Clarence E. Barnes	Sgt Robert L. Adams
Sp4 Emmett A. Dougan	Sgt Robert L. Smith
Sp4 Gyorgy S. Besze	Sgt Laurence J. Dunn
Sp4 William Graves Jr.	Sgt Henry P. Pereda

Sp4 Jimmie R. Isbell
Sp4 Howard R. Hysell
Sp4 George C. Kosovich
Sp4 Ron Nickerson
Sp4 Kenneth Vanlew
Pfc Fredrick G. Atkinson
Pfc Robert Barnes
Pfc Herbert S. Bechtel
Pfc James Brown
Pfc Max L. Brubaker
Pfc Charles E. Clark
Pfc Larry Deal
Pfc Roger W. Jenkins
Pfc Larry R. Kelm
Pfc William W. Richard
Pfc Alfred L. Spitzfaden
Pfc Robert Livingston (he died after I left)

Sp4 John Doyle
Sp4 David W. Hill
Sp4 Ronald L. Watson
Sp4 Robert Mueller
Pfc Thomas E. Clark
Pfc James Cunningham
Pfc Vernon G. Hollifield
Pfc Dick Lines
Pfc Ronald P. O'Rourke
Pfc Richard A. Recupero
Pfc Jose Rivera-Barreto
Pfc Michael Tritico
Pfc J. C. Walker Jr
Pfc Wilbert Waxton
Pfc Ronald Roth
Pfc Thomas J. Vontor

Image Citations

Cover Page. Haldane, R. (book coordinator). (1993). *First Infantry Division in Vietnam: "Big Red One."* [photo], (p. 26). Turner Publishing Company: Paducah, KY.

Fig. 1. (1965). *You are a proud soldier.* [photo].

Fig. 2. (1965). *Airborne training, Fort Benning, GA.*

Fig. 3. (1966). *Stand on your toes: Little Bitty Johnson (LBJ).*

Fig. 4. (1966). *On Patrol.*

Fig. 5. (1944). *I Met My Friends from Swampoodle: Frank J. Martin.*

Fig. 6. Haldane, R. (book coordinator). (1993). *First Infantry Division in Vietnam: "Big Red One."* Photo, (back inside cover). Turner Publishing Company: Paducah, KY.

Fig. 7. (1966). *Chuck Mundahl.*

Fig. 7. (1966). *A Visit from my Friend: Jimmy Fogarty.*

Fig. 8. Pollard, H. (2019). *Freedom's Not Free.* MSG Photography.

Fig. 9. (2019). *The Honor Flight.*

Fig. 10. (1971). *Our Wedding Picture.*

Fig. 11. Pollard, H. (2018). *Family.* MSG Photography.

Fig. 12. Pollard, H. (2019). *Family.* MSG Photography.

Fig. 13. Egan, M. (2020). *Michael Egan.*

Back Cover Page. (1913). *Fans on buildings outside Shibe Park, Philadelphia, during 1913 World Series [baseball].* Bain News Service, publisher. Retrieved from https://www.flickr.com/photos/library_of_congress/4370902668.

Just A Kid from Swampoodle to Vietnam

Edmond J. Cubbage

Made in the USA
Columbia, SC
12 June 2020